DOGS GOTTA BE IN HEAVEN

A Loving Memory of A Companion & Friend

La Vita Weaver

Copyright © 2016 La Vita Weaver
All rights reserved.

ISBN: 0692797238
ISBN 13: 9780692797235
Library of Congress Control Number: 2016917572
Dogs Gotta Be In Heaven, Alexandria, VA

DEDICATION

This book is dedicated to all animal lovers. It's dedicated to the special people who invest their love, patience and kindness to welcome animals into their hearts and into their homes. I appreciate the organizations and people who care for animals and foster pets. I extend a special thanks to those who invest their time, commitment and money to rescue animals that are abandoned, neglected, displaced or abused. I cannot forget the veterinarians who dedicate their expertise and loving care to ensure our pets are healthy and well. Thank you all for helping these beautiful creations become the special gifts God intended them to be. What a special calling!

This book is also dedicated to my adorable grandchildren who are truly gifts from above. They were my inspiration for writing this message because kids love animals too. In addition, I thank family and friends for their love and support. Last, but not least, I thank God for the opportunity of experiencing the love, joy and devotion of one of His precious creations. Nia was a beautiful Shiba Inu, who was an absolute sweetheart and part of our family for nearly fifteen years.

TABLE OF CONTENTS

Introduction	Who Can Understand?	vii
Chapter 1	An Animal Lover's Heart	1
Chapter 2	A Cherished Companion	9
Chapter 3	A Good Dog For You	18
Chapter 4	A Dog At Your Service	27
Chapter 5	A Great Fitness Partner	31
Chapter 6	A Lesson From Dogs	52
Chapter 7	A Day of Remembrance	61
Chapter 8	A Comfort From Above	66
Chapter 9	A Healing of the Heart	75
Chapter 10	A Better Life Today	92
Chapter 11	A Relationship By God	98
Chapter 12	A Celebration of Creation	104

A Special Tribute	119
About the Author	123

INTRODUCTION
WHO CAN UNDERSTAND?

All animals are God's special creations. But dogs have obvious differences. First of all, they are the only animals that bark. Early on, their voice made them useful for hunting, herding and protecting homes and property. Later people discovered that their value is much bigger than their bark. Dogs are like people in the sense that they think, reason and have unique personalities. They have real feelings and emotions. They feel pain, fear, grief, anxiety, loneliness, pleasure, and excitement. They have the ability to learn many words and commands; and they remember many people, events and experiences.

La Vita Weaver

Dogs connect to human beings in a special way. They communicate with their eyes, facial expressions, body language and a wide range of vocal sounds. They bark, growl, yelp, howl, huff, whine, whimper, and more to get their point across. They try to read our body language, voice tones, words and expressions. They even try to determine how we feel and anticipate our next actions. They become so in tuned to our emotions and sensitive to our needs. Dogs try to comfort us when we are sad, care for us when we are sick, and protect us when we are threatened. They play with us, laugh with us, and mourn with us.

Dogs are pack animals. As social creatures, they love being part of a group. That's why they easily develop a strong bond with their human families. When a family member has been away for a long period of time, you discover it's more than about food and provision. They are always ecstatic at our return. The relationship and the commitment to the pack is their motivation and priority. As naturally social beings, they are protective and loyal to their family members. And once the bond has been created, dogs remain faithful to their pack (or family).

Before we get a new dog, our excitement is obvious as friends and loved ones anticipate the arrival of our new family member. And unless you've been down that road before, death is not something that crosses your mind. A lifetime commitment to our dogs is a short 10 to 15 years. And the death of a dog can be devastating. The same intensity of love, affection and joy they bring in our lives, is the same level of traumatic grief we experience when they die. The reality is when a dog passes away, people around us respond much differently than when we lose a human family member. This is a major reason why I want to share this message.

This message is based on a tribute I wrote after Nia died. Nia, also known as "Nini", was my beautiful Shiba Inu who was a part of my family and life for nearly fifteen years. My heart deeply ached when I saw this sweet girl get sick and began to suffer. But losing Nia was heart-wrenchingly painful. After Nia passed away, I first grieved in silence. I felt as if no one would understand the intensity of my pain. So I made a conscious effort to avoid it. At least I tried. I stayed extremely busy and avoided going home at all costs. Every room in the house reminded me of Nia. And the sound of her dog tags resonated in my ears. Yet, she wasn't there.

I immediately returned to work. After work, I visited family and friends or walked up and down store aisles until closing. When I arrived home, I baked for hours. I baked for family, friends, coworkers and neighbors. I baked until I was so tired I collapsed from exhaustion. Early in the morning, I started this tiring cycle all over again. The good news was, I baked 100% all-natural muffins from scratch that were healthy and delicious. I called them "Viti's Sweeties Inspired by Nini". Everyone loved them.

At first I felt okay. At least I thought I was fine. When I stopped working, moving or baking, tears uncontrollably ran down my face. I remember gripping my chest afraid to let go and face the depths of my heartbreak. Going to work was a good distraction. But some days it was hard to concentrate on basic information and job duties. On top of that, handling daily responsibilities added to the emotional overload. Falling asleep was difficult, so I stayed up late at night looking at dogs on the internet. I must have viewed hundreds of descriptions and photos of available dogs. On the weekends I visited local shelters and animal rescues in search of the right dog. At the time, I wasn't ready for another dog. I wanted Nia back. Sadly, she was gone.

Finally, I tried to express my feelings to a close family member. She responded by comparing my relationship with Nia to people's attachments to their cars, homes or other possessions. Hearing a comparison between a living breathing creation and inanimate objects, convinced me that she did not understand. She genuinely didn't mean any harm. But she did not realize that dogs have real feelings, expressions and emotions. Unlike owning possessions, a mutual connection is formed between a person and our fury companion. They return the commitment, concern, love and affection.

The reality is when we lose a human family member, people naturally respond with concern and kind words of comfort. Friends, coworkers and neighbors extend condolences, cards, prayers and support. Losing a pet invokes a much different response. We are expected to continue life as usual and go about our normal routines. People surely do not understand when you express your grief. And God forbid if you take time off from work. The lack of empathy makes losing a pet so difficult. You feel so alone during this time of grief.

In the meantime, everything in society tells us to cover up or numb our pain. Retreating in a cocoon often seemed like a good option. But I had reached a point in my life where I pursued total wellness in every area of my life. One thing I learned is that wholeness is true wealth for a happy life. Dealing with my grief in a healthy way would be key for my hurting heart. In my despair, I found out that I was not the only one who could relate to these feelings. I was not alone. God understands.

Today, I'm truly thankful for the opportunity to share this message with you. The topics in this message are a reflection of memories of Nia and the amazing blessings that dogs bring into our lives. My prayer is that you will find peace, joy and comfort knowing how much God really cares about our relationships with our fury companions and friends. If you are considering becoming a pet owner, I share helpful advice to help you prepare for this serious commitment. If you are not ready for a pet, at the least, you will gain more insight about these special creations. Dogs are special gifts that bring so much love, joy and service in our lives. Losing one deeply hurts. But they are worth our heart's investment. Discover how loving a cherished companion is an opportunity to learn life lessons on health, happiness, purpose and passion. As an animal lover since childhood, I am absolutely amazed how these special creations help us become better human beings and embrace the true meaning of life. Enjoy!

CHAPTER 1
AN ANIMAL LOVER'S HEART

People let pets into their homes for different reasons. Animal lovers let them into our hearts. As early as I can remember, I was fascinated by animals. My love for animals extended beyond domesticated ones. Seeing a squirrel run up a tree tickled my heart. Watching the birds play tag in the sky captured my eyes. Tadpoles swimming in a pond, bunnies hopping in the grass and a family of deer in the woods aroused my curiosity. I was intrigued for hours watching animals on television or looking at pictures in books. Drawings of the magnificent beauty and strength of horses were displayed all around my bedroom. I dreamed of owning a horse one day.

La Vita Weaver

Many families in my neighborhood had dogs. Dogs ran around in fenced yards or were chained in the back yard. Dogs were commonly used to protect the home or to warn the family of an intruder. And in those days, it was not uncommon to see unleashed dogs roaming the neighborhood. I regularly greeted dogs and cats in my neighborhood. Most responded favorably. Dogs that chased boys on top of cars, allowed me to approach them and gently pet them. Cats that fearfully ran at the sight of people, slowly approached me as I mimicked their familiar meow.

My love for animals went a step further. I brought injured animals home and nursed them back to health. Others I kept as pets. My mom sacrificed her feelings to appease my love for animals. She was especially afraid of the tiny rodent-like creatures. She allowed me to bring them home as long as I promised to keep them in their cage. Otherwise, I pouted until she yielded. I had dogs, cats, gerbils, hamsters, common and tropical fish, turtles, tadpoles, frogs, insects and more. I nursed injured birds until they could freely fly. I fed roaming dogs and rescued cats taunted by neighborhood boys. To this day I remember the two animals my mom didn't let me keep. No amount of tears, begging or pouting changed her mind. As a daddy's girl, I asked my dad. Surprisingly, he told me to check with my mother. But my mom refused to live with a lizard and she said the Saint Bernard puppy would grow too big in a house with five kids. The good news was I gave the Saint Bernard to a family in my neighborhood and watched her grow into a wonderful family dog. The lizard was given to a student at school.

Friends and family felt confident I would be a veterinarian one day. That seemed like the best explanation of my attachment to animals; especially since the connection was reciprocated. Animals that saw me for the first time cheerfully approached me as if they had seen me before. Pet owners often said that their dogs or cats did not respond the same way to other people. Maybe they saw the excitement on my face and heard the friendly tone in my voice. Animals somehow knew that I had no fear and was not a threat. I believe they knew that I genuinely cared for them.

I approached many animals. I was bitten once, by the smallest dog in my neighborhood—a Chihuahua. Later, I learned that this breed is very protective. It made sense. When I walked pass his house he barked erratically. Then he squeezed his tiny body through the front gate and fearlessly ran to attack me. I tried to sweet talk him, which worked for many other dogs. But before I knew it, this tiny guard dog was digging his spiky teeth into my ankle. This incident was disturbing. But it didn't make me afraid of dogs. For instance, my older sister was chased by dogs as a kid and grew up fearing dogs. My love for animals was greater than his bark. It was bigger than his bite. I was more upset with his reaction. I loved dogs too much to kick him and hurt him. He was noisy and feisty but he was so small and cute. I just couldn't bring myself to do it. I found a simple solution to avoid this incident from ever occurring again. I ran and chose a different route home.

As I grew into an adult, my love for animals never changed. As a grown woman, I often wondered why I felt this way about animals, especially when Nia got sick. It was so painful. It was so hard to let her go. I felt I could have avoided the heartbreak if I didn't have this love for animals. The truth of the matter is losing Nia felt like I was losing a family member. I had experienced that lost before, so I know exactly what it feels like. Sometimes I felt strange or was made to feel that way by others. I was no longer a little girl. I was an adult who had beautiful children and adorable grandchildren. Yet, I still had a strong connection to animals.

At some point our children grow up and become independent. They eventually dress themselves, feed themselves and take care of themselves. They fly out of the nest and move on with their own lives and families. Our pets are always there. They will never be able to feed themselves or get a fresh bowl of water. They will never be able to groom themselves, brush their teeth or drive to the veterinarian's office. Every day, for the rest of their lives, they rely on our care. They become a major part of our heart and an integral part of our daily routine. They depend on us, but we also develop an unbreakable bond with them. They are our "forever children". Their lives are so intertwined with ours as if they become part of our DNA. Losing one feels like you lost a part of yourself. Not only that, it hurts so badly because you lost part of the goodness in your life.

When I talked about Nia after she passed away, I introduced the conversation with, "I know I shouldn't feel this way..." or "I know she's only a dog..." Later I heard other animal lovers make similar comments after losing a pet. We try to dismiss or deny our true feelings. Or we are not comfortable expressing how we really feel. And we have our reasons. Avoiding criticism or being misunderstood seems like a better option. Plus over the years, I've heard people make negative comments. I've heard statements like "People who love animals have a void in their lives." I thought that was ridiculous. Before I was old enough to experience life's hurts, pain, rejection, and disappointments, animals captivated my heart.

Growing up, it was five children in my household. We were very close. We played board games and jumped rope. We played kick ball, battled over jacks, and baked on our Easy Bank Oven. Before the basement was finished, we hung ropes from the ceiling, tied to an old tire, and swung like we were on an outdoor swing set. This was the alternative when it was too cold to swing on the one in the backyard. We had so much fun! Yet I still loved animals. I heard others say that people who love animals don't love people. I could never relate to that statement either. I've always adored children. I had three and wanted more; but life's circumstances changed those plans. Nevertheless, I genuinely love grown folks too. Today, I have healthy relationships with family, friends, co-workers and others. People have a natural tendency to criticize what they don't understand.

Throughout my life, some of the most kind, tender-hearted, and caring people I've ever met love animals. To the contrary, some of the most unkind, mean and insensitive people I've met didn't care for animals. Obviously, it's not fair to stereotype everyone into the same category. And yes, we see people who struggle with unhealthy addictions to food, drugs, alcohol, possessions or even animals. But this is not the case with animal lovers. We look out for the best interest of animals. We avoid putting them in a position where they cannot be properly taken care of or hurt. Animals are not collectible items or mere possessions to fulfill emptiness or a void in our lives. Our pets are part of our family.

After Nia died, I finally got my answer. Our love for animals is from above. Animals are part of God's magnificent creation too. In the beginning of creation, God was well pleased when He created them and said it was "good". Not only that, God created animals from the same dust of the earth He used to form mankind. And the same gift of life that flows in their lungs, flows in our lungs and circulates oxygenated blood throughout our bodies. Human beings are connected to animals by the life-giving breath of God. Animal lovers are sensitive to this divine flow.

Consider this: If people did not love animals who would take care of them and welcome them into their homes? Who would rescue the abused and neglected? Who would care for the abandoned ones left alone? Who would foster those waiting for a loving home? Who would care what happens to those whose natural habitats are destroyed or those who are part of disasters with nowhere to go? To take it further some animals are abused and neglected and spend their entire existence in horrifying circumstances. Some dogs spend their entire lives in crates used as puppy machines for greed. They are discarded or killed when they no longer produce a profit. Or they are discarded like waste when they get sick from their filthy living conditions. Sadly, dogs are beaten and intentionally starved to make them vicious. Then they are forced to fight where they are badly hurt, maimed or killed. These animals need someone to fight on their behalf. They need passionate hearts who genuinely care.

We all can agree that we should love and care for the well-being of all human beings. That's a given. As Creator of the universe, love is God's greatest attribute. Everything He created was motivated by His amazing love. Then He pours His love into our hearts to overflow and make a difference on the earth. And please do not misconstrue this message. In no way am I suggesting that people who don't love animals lack the love of God in their hearts. But keep in mind, God is infinite. We are created beings, therefore we are finite. Our understanding of God's wisdom, knowledge and attributes is limited. While on this earth, we could never embrace the full magnitude of the depths, heights, and measure of His incredible love for all creation. Therefore, loving animals simply allows us to experience another part of the heart of God. *He* was the first animal lover.

CHAPTER 2
A CHERISHED COMPANION

Dogs have been called man's best friend for a reason. They are fun, loyal, show unconditional love, and make great companions. They stay by your side, until they take their last breath. They always protect their family or at least warn loved ones of apparent danger. Dogs never criticize you and they accept you just as you are. A dog won't let a day go by without showing you he's happy to be in your presence. They greet you with a jump, a leap, a wagging tail or running around that make you laugh and smile. Imagine being greeted with the same energy and excitement every single day. Their personalities, playfulness, and tricks entertain us for hours and add so much joy in our lives. Dogs are naturally affectionate. When you feel down they comfort you with a rub or a kiss, or place their heads in your lap. They are so in tuned to our feelings and emotions and will try to predict or emulate our moods.

I distinctly remember Morgan, Yun Yun, Bruno, Brutus, Conan and Cierra. All of our dogs were special. Each of them had a unique personality and somehow made a difference in my life. But my relationship with Nia was exceptionally special. First of all, she was my first dog in over ten years. After my beautiful Pomeranian, Cierra died, I avoided getting another dog, especially since her sister passed away a year earlier. The pain of losing an animal was too much. So I admired dogs from afar. Then years later, my youngest daughter was deeply distressed when her guinea pig died. One month Babyboy was active and alive. The month of his fifth birthday, he took his last breath and died. I was going to get another one. But she said guinea pigs died too soon. We hadn't had a dog since she was born. Her birthday was approaching and I knew a puppy would be the perfect gift to uplift her heart.

When I visited Nia and her seven littermates, Nia was special right from the start. As soon as I entered the room we made direct eye contact. She wouldn't take her eyes off of me. I intentionally swayed from right to left and walked away. Her bright beautiful brown eyes followed me. Then I noticed she didn't react the same way to other people in the room. Then she jumped and leaped, until she kept my attention. Her slightly different appearance made her stand out from the others. She was petite, had a narrower face and round eyes. Her ears were larger and the tips were still bent over (They would later stand up). I thought she was one of the cutest puppies I had ever seen. Not only did her physical appearance grab my attention, she seemed so dainty and feminine. This is why later "Girlie" would be one of her nicknames. She looked like a little girl and had a pep in her step like she knew it.

The other seven puppies looked more alike; the only difference was their color. Half were reddish-brown and Nia and the others were tan and black. They were all adorable. But it was something special about Nia. When she was taken out of the crate, she excitedly hopped and leaped like a bunny rabbit. I laughed so hard I cried. I never saw a dog hop like that before. She was upbeat, happy and full of life right from the start. A big smile covered her face the entire time. We played for over an hour and had an immediate connection. There was no reason to see another puppy. Nia chose me. Later I learned that the physical attributes that caught my attention were imperfections for her breed. But God knew she would be perfect for me. Nia was the sweetest, smartest, happiest, most lovable, and adorable animal I had ever seen. Later, people who didn't necessarily care for animals would love her too.

Nia came home November 17, 2001, several days before LaTia's birthday. To say LaTia was ecstatic would be a huge understatement. No words can express the level of excitement and joy that was on her face. She looked as if she had seen the face of God. And as I predicted, she said the puppy was the best birthday present ever. Nia was nine weeks old. When she saw LaTia, she responded the same as earlier. She hopped like a bunny rabbit and leaped so high I thought she would hurt her legs at landing. She was happy to be part of our family.

Next, we had to choose a name. That wasn't too difficult. That same week, LaTia and I watched a popular comedy that featured a petite beautiful co-star named "Nia". LaTia and I looked at each other and screamed, "Nia!" We agreed it was the perfect name. We later found out the actress also loves dogs. I didn't know how she would feel if she knew a puppy was given her name. But if she knew how beautiful, adorable and well-loved the puppy was, she could never be offended. Later, my middle daughter suggested the same name because "Nia" somewhat rhymed with "LaTia". Nia nicknames would later be "Nini", "Girlie" and "Girlie in my worlie". These different names never confused Nia. Each name accompanied different activities, rewards and affection. And she welcomed them all.

Not only was Nia upbeat and loving, she was so smart and had a great memory. She remembered family member's names and knew many words. She loved learning. She was easy to train, good with children and enjoyed outings with family and friends. She was energetic and agile and people often compared her abilities and talents to a show dog. Her characteristics and independence suited our family and lifestyle well. What is most memorable about Nia is her natural good-nature. She was an absolute sweetheart. People often said she was so loving and well-behaved because she was surrounded by love. She was that way from the moment I brought her home. Our love nurtured what was already part of her personality and make-up. Nia was a sweetheart, but she boldly and fearlessly protected our home. And during walks she reacted to strangers based on our voice tone and body language. She intently watched people until she was sure they were not a threat. Then she became more comfortable and friendly.

Nia loved LaTia, but she was very attached to me. Initially, that was the reason why I avoided getting another dog for so long. Investing emotions in animals seemed too painful. But I had forgotten how much joy dogs bring in our lives. Nia proved to be worth my heart's investment. From the first day I saw her, that gleam in her beautiful brown eyes never changed. She always tried to read my emotions, body language, expressions, tone of voice and feelings. When I spoke, she stared at my mouth as if she was reading my lips or trying to understand my words. And she anticipated the next command, trick or challenge. She was always alert and willing to discover something new. My daughters stated that she had my personality and even developed my idiosyncrasies. At times it seemed as if she knew me better than I knew myself. She studied all of my habits and always seemed to be aware of my next actions.

In the past, I've heard people say that dogs are so loyal because we feed them and give them water. In other words, they have no choice if they want their needs met. Early on, my daughter had the responsibility to feed Nia and give her water. They were playmates, walking partners and they ran together regularly. This relationship didn't prevent Nia from becoming extremely attached to me. My daughter claimed that I babied Nia, that's why she treated me like her mother. She was such a sweet loving girl, I couldn't help but to return the love. As a young puppy, Nia embraced my role as "Mommy" in the house and affectionately responded to my name. Our close relationship worked out for good. When children grow up, it's common for the child's dog to stay with the parents. This is exactly what happened. Years later when my daughter left home, Nia happily stayed with me, but always looked forward to LaTia's visits.

Nia was a wonderful family dog and companion. We drove to different states and stayed overnight in pet-friendly hotels. Besides road trips, she was so well behaved we regularly visited family and friends. Eager to ride in the car, she would anticipate which family member or friend we would visit. When she heard "grandma", she knew we were going to my mother's house. To say my mom loved and adored Nia, is putting it lightly. My mom looked forward to our visits too. People we visited for the first time were always surprised. And interestingly, people who never allowed animals in their home, welcomed Nia. She was very polite and would ask permission before she entered certain rooms or approached someone. And if food was within her reach, she would wait for permission or my nod to proceed.

All of my children and grandchildren adored Nia. We had Nia before I had grandchildren so she knew each of them since birth. And she was so good with kids. When they pulled her tail or annoyed her, her reaction was amazing to watch. She gently grabbed the child's hand with her mouth and carefully removed it from her body. And when they tried to ride on her back when they were toddlers, she lowered her body to the ground to ease them off. If a child insisted on taunting her, she left the room. She refused to hurt a child and handled my grandbabies with tender care.

Whenever I traveled without Nia, she sat at the front door awaiting my return. During one of my trips, my daughter called extremely concerned. She thought Nia was sick because she stopped eating and drinking. It was the first time I was gone for a week. As soon as I walked through the door, Nia leaped like I had been reincarnated and wouldn't stop greeting me with hugs and kisses. Later, her appetite returned. She excitably grabbed her bowls and asked for food and water. Later when I traveled, she ate and drank a little more. But she always remained planted at the front door, until my return.

I never had to scold Nia. The one day I raised my voice at her, hurt me more than it hurt her. I had a frustrating day and was quite agitated. After I raised my voice, what happened next hurt me. Nia walked over to the edge of the sofa and hid her face behind the sofa. To this day, I don't know if raising my voice hurt her feelings or if she thought she disappointed me. I apologized to my girlie and she easily forgave me. Later we played like the incident never happened. Nia was truly a cherished companion and such a "good girl" and she knew that name too.

CHAPTER 3
A GOOD DOG FOR YOU

As stated earlier, my heart was captured right from the start by a beautiful puppy that hopped like a bunny rabbit. Plus her tan and black coloring was similar to one of my favorite childhood dogs, a handsome German Shepherd named Brutus. Then her different appearance made her stand out from her littermates. Like most people, I was not familiar with her breed. More people are familiar with the Japanese Akita. The Akita is large and powerfully built dog with a thick plush shining coat. He is a strikingly stunning dog. But he was originally bred for fighting, so his temperament has to be watched. An Akita co-starred in the movie, "Hachi: A Dog's Tale". The movie is based on a true story. It is about a college professor that forms a lasting bond with a dog he finds at the train station. When Hachi grew up, he met the professor at the train station every day when he got off from work. After the college professor died, every day for nine years Hachi returned to the train station awaiting the professor's arrival. This shows the extent of the commitment and loyalty of a faithful companion and friend.

Nia was a Japanese Shiba Inu. They are similar in appearance to the Akita, but are one of the smaller Japanese spritz breeds (ranging up to 25 pounds). Their colors includes red, black, black and tan, tan, and brindle, with the same plush feel to the coat. Like the Akita, they are good looking dogs. But their temperament is not aggressive. During walks, Nia caught people's attention as they complimented her beauty and youthful appearance. Most people were not familiar with her breed. They often assumed she was either an Akita, Husky or German Shepherd puppy.

Displaying her breed's primary characteristics, Nia was very intelligent and loved to learn. She didn't make much noise, but was an excellent companion and watch dog. She had an energetic cheerful personality and loved joining family activities. Nia was perfect for our family. However, this breed has its challenges too. Surprisingly, Nia could be strong-willed and stubborn. LaTia experienced it many times. But it made sense. As pack animals, dogs respect the hierarchy of the group. They quickly recognize the family order. Nia considered LaTia an equal or a younger sibling. She sometimes ignored LaTia, yet immediately responded to my same command. Or she pulled LaTia during walks, yet followed my strides. What was most shocking is LaTia insisted that Nia showed her teeth if she didn't get her way. I never saw this side. But LaTia often tried to cuddle Nia. A Shiba Inu is far from a lap dog. They show affection in their own way and they will kiss you and leap for joy to greet you. And they seem to have some cat-like characteristics. They are very independent and don't like to be held. Nia was agitated whenever LaTia invaded her personal space and she often struggled to leap out of LaTia's arms.

I've heard people say that their Shiba Inu was hard to train because of the stubbornness. Nia had to know who was in charge or she would take control. She was very smart and could easily figure things out. I had no problems. Nia responded well to being rewarded and being called "good girl". Her favorite pillow displayed the words "good dog" and a halo is over the "g" in the word "good". I bought it when she was a puppy and she lived up to the title. The pillow is still in the rocking chair in my bedroom. When Nia was younger, consistency and developing a routine was important for successful training. Sticking to a schedule helped a lot and made training easy. Family and friends were amazed how she remembered so much and was able to learn something new so quickly.

Nia was such a great dog, but if I had to complain about this breed, it would be the shedding. Nia's fur was soft and shiny, but the thick undercoat shed regularly. I love a very clean house, so that drove me crazy in the beginning. I worked extra hard to eliminate all signs of fur in the house. I purchased all types of combs, brushes and dog rakes until I found what worked best. The indoor heating system we use today seemed to contribute to more shedding. Thankfully, her fur was soft and plush and easy to clean up. My daily brushings, combined with blowouts by a groomer reduced shedding and helped cut back on the cleanup. Other than that, Nia was a very clean dog. She didn't have a "doggy" smell and was easy to take care of. If I believed in luck, I really lucked out with Nia. I had such an amazing experience that I hope to get another Shiba Inu one day, preferably a black and tan little girl. I know I can never replace Nia. Each dog has its individual personality. But the breed's major characteristics worked well with my personality and lifestyle. And Nia was truly a blessing.

When I chose a dog in the past, I didn't necessarily look for a specific breed. Most of our childhood dogs were German Shepherds, so they were my preference. Other than that, if a puppy was cute and adorable or needed a good home, I brought it home. Every dog was not the best choice. But like a mother with a challenging child, I worked with the dog. Now I know choosing a dog takes careful consideration. Owning a dog is a serious commitment that will last the animal's lifetime, approximately 10-15 years. Dogs bring a lot of joy, fun, affection and companionship in our lives. But they require a lot of time and attention.

Before getting a dog, you have to consider if you have the time and energy to commit to the care of the dog. Next, you have to consider the cost. The cost depends on whether you get a dog from a breeder or adopt a dog from an animal rescue or local shelter. The price ranges from hundreds to thousands, with adoption as the less costly option. If a dog is a gift, there are still many expenses to consider. Humans need regular checkups and vaccinations and dogs do too. There are veterinarian's expenses to consider. A puppy need vaccinations and spaying or neutering. Adult dogs require booster shots. And all dogs require heartworm, flea and tick prevention medications, which is a monthly expense. Regular teeth cleanings for good dental hygiene is another expense.

The dog's size and appetite will determine how much you spend on food. The type of food affects the price, especially if you want a good brand. A special food, such as one that's easily digestible for sensitive stomachs, costs more. In addition to food, dogs need food and water bowls, a leash and collar, toys and training pads, depending on the breed and your preference. Next, you have to determine whether to buy a crate, bedding, gate or dog pen. And if you want to protect your furniture, shoes, clothes and household items you need a supply of chew toys. Like human babies, puppies' gums burn and hurt during teething. Plus they discover the world with their mouths. They chew on almost anything they can sink their teeth into. And depending on how badly the puppy is teething will determine how often you buy new toys. Human babies gum their toys. Our fury babies bite through their toys or rip them apart. In this case you have to replace them frequently for the puppy's health and safety. Older dogs like to enjoy playtime with toys as well.

Other expenses may be a pet sitter, boarding and grooming, depending on the breed. At the least, dogs need regular baths, brushing, nail clippings and their teeth brushed. You can learn to do this yourself. Then you have determine who will care for the dog if you work late, have a special event or travel out of town. Once you work through these details, unexpected medical expenses may arise. Like people, dogs get sick and will need emergency veterinarian visits. Unexpected animal hospital visits, prescriptions, blood work and medical procedures are other expenses that can quickly add up.

In addition to the financial responsibility, time and commitment you want to find out if the dog is good for your lifestyle and family. For example, you wouldn't want to get an active dog that needs a lot of exercise if you are not active. Or if you want a dog to run with, choose an active breed. Take your time to find the right dog for you. Find out basic information like temperament, adult size, grooming, exercise needs and prone health conditions. Others considerations are expected life-span, living space recommendations and if the breed is good for an individual or is more suited for a family. It's also important to know which breeds are naturally more aggressive. Some breeds make good watch dogs, but are not good for small children, other pets or guests. And then find out if the breed is allowed in your community or development.

There are hundreds of breeds of dogs and an unlimited variety of different mixes. Mix breeds make excellent family pets as well. They generally live longer and have less known health conditions than purebreds. In addition to different breeds and mixes, each individual dog has a unique personality. Meeting the dog in advance will let you see how the dog interacts with you. Nia clearly stood out from her seven littermates. She was the most outgoing and energetic puppy in the litter. She remained that way throughout her life. As a fitness trainer, her energy matched my lifestyle and she would help LaTia and I stay active for years down the road.

Other considerations are how long the dog will be alone during the day and who will help you take care of the dog. Think about if you have time to invest in a puppy or do you prefer an adult dog who is already trained. Generally speaking, puppies require a lot more work. Like toddlers, they are curious about the world around them and will get into almost everything. They are full of non-stop energy and will chew on almost anything, including your household plants. They need to be house broken, socialized, and properly trained. Although Nia's breed is independent and not demanding, we invested the time training her as a puppy. The attention, exercise and care kept her happy and made our lives easier.

Then some dogs are more demanding than others. They need an experienced owner or someone who is patient and have the time to work with the dog. Others are very active and require more yard space to burn energy. When a dog is not used for its breed's purpose, he may show destructive or annoying behavior, such as excessive barking, aggression, excessive chewing or biting. Dogs feel lonely, bored and anxious if neglected and ignored. Like children, they begin to act out with behavioral problems. Dogs need attention and care. They need to be properly trained to adjust to their new lifestyle. Most dogs are trainable, if you are willing to invest the time.

Today, many dogs are house dogs and don't have the inside space to freely run to burn energy. At the very least they need daily walks, playful activities and socialization to be healthy. They need to develop healthy relationships with people and other dogs. With all of these considerations, we can better understand why so many dogs are surrendered to animal shelters or abandoned. They were not necessarily "bad" dogs. People take dogs home, without carefully considering if they are prepared for the type of dog or the long-term commitment. In some cases, the dog was not properly matched with the right person, family or environment. Or they did not have the proper time, care and attention to help them grow into a healthy member of the family. Having a dog is a wonderful experience. But it's a huge commitment. If these factors are not carefully considered in advance, you may find yourself overwhelmed with a responsibility you were not prepared to handle. You may find a dog that you think is good for you; but consider if you are a good fit for the dog.

CHAPTER 4

A DOG AT YOUR SERVICE

Originally bred for hunting small birds and game, Shiba Inus are one of the smaller spritz breeds from Japan. But they are known for their spirited and bold personality. This made sense. Nia was extremely alert and could spot someone approaching the house before I could hear a sound. She would not tolerate the idea of an invader on her own property. She was fearlessly ready to protect her family. Not only that, she was agile and could jump incredibly high. She was always eager to perform some type of task or activity. Fetch was one of her favorite games and she loved flying in the air to catch a Frisbee. Late evenings, she routinely grabbed my slippers when I got home from work. When I grabbed a movie, she grabbed the remote control off of the television stand. Intently observing my face, she eagerly awaited the next command, trick, game or job to do.

Like Nia, most modern dogs are kept as pets. But our canine companions were originally bred for a specific purpose. Dogs were bred for many reasons. Their intuition and keen sense of danger, sight, smell and sound are useful today. Over the years, not only have dogs been part of our families, they have become part of the human workforce. They serve man in a variety of fields. Our beloved companions deserve recognition for the help they provide mankind. I want to share some of the ways that G-o-d has allowed the d-o-g to be a blessing to the human race.

It's fascinating to see the many ways dogs have developed to help human beings. Dogs have been commonly used as guard dogs to protect the home. But dogs can do a lot more than bark and ward off a prowling stranger. 0ver the many years, dogs have been used to detect drugs and explosives for the military, police department and at airports to keep the public safe and protect the nation. Dogs are actively used in the police force to enforce public order and for search and rescue missions. Missing children, adults and cadavers have been located by dogs. Tracking dogs help find lost victims, animals and criminals. Water rescue dogs have been used to help people in danger of drowning. These dogs swim out to a person and gently grab the victim to bring them back to shore.

Service dogs are commonly used to assist people with various disabilities. Guide dogs help the visually impaired and hearing dogs help the hearing impaired. Mobile assistance dogs help the physically handicapped with household tasks such as opening doors and grabbing things that they need. Health facilities and nursing homes use dogs to bring cheer and comfort to the sick to facilitate healing. And dogs' powerful ability of smell is used in hospitals to detect certain illnesses and disease.

Our canine companions are used in therapy in homes, hospitals, and nursing homes to help people recover from illnesses or to provide warnings. For instance, dogs have been trained to alert people with epilepsy prior to a seizure to give them time to call for help. Some dogs signal a family member by barking to indicate when certain conditions require immediate attention. Autistic children have been known to respond favorably to dogs, when they otherwise would not respond to human interaction.

Dogs are used in programs to help children learn how to read. The child reads aloud to the dog. Dogs don't criticize, laugh, belittle or care about what the child wears. They are happy to have the company and attention. Their positive disposition increases the child's confidence and creates a stress-free learning environment. In addition to reading, dogs can help children develop healthy relationships with others by boosting their self-esteem. And taking care of a dog can teach children responsibility as they grow into healthy adults. They learn a routine that creates discipline in their lives. Dogs also help children learn how to have a giving heart, how to share with others and how to be kind, sensitive and affectionate.

Dogs have been used for our pleasure and enjoyment and have serviced society for a very long time. Let's not forget those who are used in herding, sledding, racing, hunting, guarding and even mascots. Then our talented fury friends have entertained the nation for many years on television and in the movies. Show dogs have graciously displayed their natural beauty and attributes as they pranced across the platform for our admiration. Dogs are truly a gift to mankind. They need us; but we need them too. Thank God for dogs at our service!

CHAPTER 5
A GREAT FITNESS PARTNER

Can you imagine having the cure for a deadly disease? Unfortunately, people refuse the cure every day. It's not in a bottle. And you don't have to get a prescription to use it. It's absolutely free—exercise. For years we have heard the many benefits of exercise and a healthy lifestyle. Exercise reduces the risk of illnesses and diseases and helps you lose weight and get in shape. Regular physical activity reduces stress, anxiety and depression; gives you more energy and vitality; and helps you sleep better, feel better and look younger longer. There are so many benefits of exercise that it is impossible to name them all. If we could place its benefits in a bottle, people would fight to own its rights. This bottle would be invaluable, as the cure to enjoy a better quality of life. People would quickly realize that health is true wealth.

In addition, employers, CEO's, shareholders, executives and managers would support its distribution. Unfortunately, some companies fail to recognize that supporting a healthy heart is business smart. Healthy employees are happier; they stay longer, and have less job absenteeism and medical crises due to stress. In turn, they are more productive and can achieve overall goals for company success. An employee health program would be a win-win situation. Employees will have the energy and stamina to perform their daily activities with ease. Healthy employees benefit the long-term stability and growth of the organization. Realistically, if most people want to stay healthy, they have to find their own exercise program, fitness center or exercise partner or trainer.

We learned that dogs make great companions and loyal friends, but they also make great fitness partners. They can help us achieve powerful health benefits. They help adults and children stay active. We can take advantage of their energy and briskly walk them or run with them depending on the breed. When you take advantage of their non-stop energy, you both will be happier and healthier. They also love to play catch and run around the yard or house to be chased. So you can put on your tennis shoes and run and have some fun. Dogs can help you get moving for a healthy body and mind.

While mentioning exercise, I have to share the story of one of my favorite childhood dogs. I often call each of my animals my favorite. They all were special. Each of them had a unique personality and made a difference in my life. Nia played a major role in my adult years. My relationship with Morgan influenced my childhood years. Summers were exciting when I was in elementary school. As the middle child, I spent many summers visiting my mother's first cousin, Mary. I always had a great time. We went on road trips and visited amusement parks and museums. We went shopping and ate at good restaurants. I always felt special visiting her home. As the middle of five children, I had a younger brother and sister and an older brother and sister. I believe that's why my mom and dad allowed me to visit Mary's house by myself. It was my special time. And I always came home excited about the fun we had.

This one particular summer was the best ever. To my surprise they adopted a dog name "Morgan". He would later be called "Mr. Morgan" because people said he behaved like a little man. He was a small mix-breed young adult dog. If I had to describe his appearance, he had the beautiful reddish chestnut color of an Irish Setter, but was similar in size and appearance to a Beagle. His muscular build showed he was mixed with another breed or he developed his muscular build from his active lifestyle. Morgan loved to run!

That particular summer I didn't want to go anywhere where Morgan couldn't go. I wanted to spend every waking moment with him. We ate together, played together, slept together and we ran together. We ran up and down the street. We ran around the block. We ran until neither one of us could run no more. At one time, he smoked me. By the end of the summer, I had more stamina to hang in with him. I could at least finish the race. Then finally the summer was over too soon. As I packed my suitcase, I felt sad as I prepared to go home. The new school year was about to start. At the end of the previous summers, I was excited to go school shopping. This time new clothes were not important. The thought of leaving Morgan behind preoccupied my mind.

When my parents arrived to pick me up, I could not let Morgan go. Then Mary gently smiled and handed me his leash. She gave me a big hug and told me to take my dog home. I jumped and screamed and shouted. We had family dogs in the past. But I couldn't believe that Morgan would be my very own dog. I guess she had to first check with my parents.

Plus she watched me take care of him the entire summer. This was the best gift I ever had. I could not get home fast enough to show my brothers and sisters. And I could not wait to go to school to tell my friends.

After I brought him home we remained inseparable. During those days, dogs were not always walked on leashes. Morgan had a collar with tags, but I rarely used his leash. He followed me everywhere and stayed by my side. Today I realize he thought he was my protector. He knew that I was a child. When I came home from school, he always awaited my arrival. We went to the store together and shared our favorite snacks. He loved the red, white and blue bomb pop (that looks like a rocket) and chocolate covered malt balls. After we snacked, it was time for our daily run. When I first started racing Morgan, I was so far behind him. As time went on, the gap became smaller until I became a faster runner. I developed very strong legs and looked like an athlete. We must have ran together for years. We ran to the store and around the neighborhood. We ran up and down hills and we ran to visit my friends. Then I started racing the boys in my neighborhood. I smoked all of them. Then I joined the flag football team and outran all my opponents as a running back. Years later, I joined the track team in junior high school and did extremely well. I won many races and my name was in the papers. People often wondered how I did so well with little training. Racing Morgan was my training and I continued running during high school years.

My passion for fitness continued into my adult years. When I went into the police academy, I broke all of the female records in running, push-ups, sit-ups and all physical fitness tests. My scores exceeded many of the men's performance. I was the first female awarded the Physical Fitness Award in the police department's history. At the police academy's graduation, people were shocked when the MC announced all of the records that were broken. Heads in the crowd turned, as people guessed which physically fit male officer won the award. After my name was called, the crowd went wild with applause. I received a standing ovation when they saw a petite female stand to accept the award. As I looked out across the cheering crowd, I remembered my fitness partner, Morgan.

In the police academy I was in the running for the academic award. Later the department's defensive tactics and fitness trainer stated that they had never seen a woman demonstrate that type of ability and strength in physical fitness and defensive tactics. They agreed that the fitness award was more appropriate. After I left the police department, my passion for healthy living led me back to school. I went to college and majored in biology and health. I graduated with high honors, won first place in the Student Speaking Competition and represented my graduating class as the Student Commencement Speaker. Many years later, the keynote speaker's message still resonates in my mind. She addressed how the happiest successful people are those who pursue their passion. Today, she is a journalist, author and CEO of a television network. Her inspirational message influenced my decision to follow my heart.

My passion led to a career to inspire others to live healthier. I became a personal trainer and fitness counselor and CPR instructor. Over the years, it seemed as if I've taught hundreds of classes and trained so many clients. In addition, I produced and hosted "Eternally Fit" an award-winning local cable health and fitness program. I produced Hallelujah! Aerobics For Body and Spirit, the first praise aerobic workout of its kind. My story aired on the well-known "700 Club", on the popular *TBN,* and on radio and was in national publications. As co-host of the popular *TBN* show "TotaLee Fit", I shared the joy of fitness internationally, with 8-Times Mr. Olympia. I was blessed to teach healthy living at workshops, conferences and special events across the nation.

During health and fitness workshops, money was always mentioned as a challenge for healthy living. At one of my workshops, a young mother asked how she could focus on eating healthier when she worried if she had enough food to feed her family. I gave my best effort to provide healthier alternatives for a limited income. But I will never forget the distress on her face and the helplessness in her trembling voice. I shared how to set aside time to exercise, but financial challenges zapped her strength. Her story was one of the many that I repeatedly heard over the years. Broccoli and carrots don't cross your mind, when you are concerned about feeding your family for the day. Regular exercise is not a concern when you are praying for the energy to work a second job. These stories pulled on my heart strings and revealed a much bigger challenge for the nation's health dilemma. Financial struggles cause people to have different priorities. It is difficult to focus on healthier choices when struggling to make ends meet and while weighed down by the stress of debt.

With this in mind, I realized that knowledge is good. But I thought the best way to truly understand the extent of people's financial challenges would be from first-hand experience. With careful consideration, I pursued a career in the financial industry to learn more about the economy and money management. There I learned how people of different socioeconomic statuses, races and cultures view and manage money on a day-to-day basis. I also gained insight of the priorities, spending habits, and financial concerns of different communities. Working in the financial industry confirmed what I experienced personally and in the physically fitness industry. There is a direct correlation between physical health and financial wellness. There is clearly a health and wealth connection.

In order to effectively battle the nation's health crisis we must address financial health. The pain and strain of money problems cause real physiological and emotional symptoms. The emotional burden of debt and the inability to pay your bills lead to worry, anxiety, stress and unhealthy habits that deteriorate your mood, attitude and overall well-being. Many people feel helpless and hopeless, which leads to depression and neglect of their health. Some people overeat to sooth the discomfort. Others toss and turn all night unable to sleep; while still some lose their appetite leading to undesirable weight loss. The lack of resources can significantly contribute to the deterioration of one's total well-being.

Clearly, it is not God's will for us to struggle with financial strongholds that prevent us from functioning effectively in our homes, on our jobs, and in our communities. Therefore, financial literacy and learning how to use money wisely is another important aspect of healthy living.

Just as eating right and exercising improve our physical health; reducing debt and better money management improve our day to day living. Every decision and life's goals are related to our finances. For instance, pursuing higher education and buying a home require money. Planning a wedding or retirement requires personal finances. Going on vacation, joining a fitness center and eating healthier take budgeting. Simply meeting our basic needs such as food, housing, clothes, and transportation takes money management. And we learned earlier that having a dog requires money to cover the expenses of taking care of one. The bottom line is money is a tool to enjoy our desires, achieve our goals and build a better quality of life. But it is a two-fold process. First, we need a plan to earn enough money to meet our basic needs and to pursue our goals. Then we need to know how to properly spend, save and invest money to reap the full benefits of planning a better life.

In addition to learning about financial fitness, returning to the everyday workforce allowed me to experience another obstacle to healthy living. On top of taking care of a family and trying to make ends meet, workplace issues cause major challenges. We spend most of our waking hours at work with co-workers, managers and customers. Unfortunately, issues on the job can lead to emotional distress and frustration. Experiencing tension for the majority of your day places undue stress on the body and mind. Stress has been linked to many illnesses and diseases. The ill-effects of stress can significantly damage your health and overall well-being. Stress causes real physiological symptoms such as headaches, stomach aches and other bodily aches and pains. The body responds to the emotional weight of the distress. The emotional upset of stress also leads to overeating or bingeing, which quickly adds on extra pounds and other symptoms that deteriorate your health.

Over the years, I've taught how eating right and exercising are great ways to improve your overall health and reduce the anxiety associated with the stressors of life. Learning about other obstacles of healthy living added more fuel to my passion. Let's talk about passion for a moment. Passion has reciprocal qualities. Passion empowers us to achieve our goals while inspiring others to reach their full potential. Passion is often activated by personal pain and trials or by witnessing the mistreatment, struggles or injustice of others. And it comes with a price. As matter of fact, it is often the crises in our lives that reveal the passion in our hearts. The place of our greatest pain or struggle is often the place of our greatest passion.

Life is full of challenges, disappointments and uncertainties that cause discouragement and doubt. Like the best investments, if your passion is going to work for you, you have to hang in there for the long run. Once you discover your passion, keep the vision before you. Write the vision down and describe what drives you to want to pursue it. Review it periodically to keep the fire alive and burning. And make sure you tune out negative people and doubters. A positive attitude will help you hold on to your passion. Passion helps you use the gift God put inside of you to the best of your ability.

Yes, everyone has a special ability from God. Everyone was created with a specific purpose in mind. And yes, there is greatness inside of you. Your gift may not be my gift, but *you* have a gift. My gift may not be your gift, but I have a gift. God never intended for the competition in our society that leads to envy, jealousy, backbiting and all types of lies and resentment. The Bible is clear that every human being was created in God's image and was fearfully and wonderfully made. Therefore, you don't have to compare yourself to others or envy their gifts, talents, abilities or accomplishments.

Many people spend most of their lives searching for greatness. It is time to tap into the greatness you already have on the inside. No one can be you like you. So be the best you, you can possibly be. Then strive to become better every day as you learn and grow along the way. And know what God has for you is for you. Have faith in God and enjoy the journey one day at a time. Know that He is preparing you for something greater. See, talents and abilities can take you where you want to go. Character helps you overcome the challenges once you arrive. And character is only developed with growth. The Bible says that *your* gift will make room for *you* and bring *you* before great men. Our gifts lead us on the path to our destiny. So follow the passion in your heart, step out by faith and place your trust in God.

If you don't know what your gifts are, ask God. And He will reveal them to you at the right time. In addition, there are many workshops designed to help you identify your gifts. Other people can also help you discover what they are. Your gifts are not what you think you do well. They are designed to help others. Therefore, friends, family members, co-workers and other people are good sources to find out what you do well. Or they can tell you how you best inspire others.

The fierce competition we see today that rips existing relationships apart and prevents others from occurring was never God's desire for His children. This world is full of a diversity of causes and people. So surely it is big enough for each of us to share our ambitions, gifts and talents somewhere and with someone. God is all about relationships. And a healthy relationship with God helps us have healthy relationships with others. When we seek God for health and wholeness we can willingly learn from one another. And we can encourage one another, embrace each other's differences and support each other's goals for greater good.

If God gave each of us gifts, have you ever wondered why some people are more successful using them than others? Gifts are wonderful. But once we discover what they are, we need to know how to effectively use them. As physical exercise strengthens our muscles to work harder, the more you exercise your gifts the more they develop and mature. And passion enhances our gifts to reach their full potential. Passion kindles the flame in our hearts. Passion energizes you to perform in such a way that no trial, tribulation or pain can stop you. Passion captivates the attention of those in its presence. When you pursue your passion, you will give it the best you've got because you love what you do. And when your passion moves you, it will move others too. Passion fuels success.

As you pursue your passion, get advice from an expert or someone who is where you want to be. Do not limit yourself by seeking the same opportunities as others or sticking to one area or community. Be daring. Tap into diverse resources and arenas. Take the initiative to reach wider and higher. Get a broader perspective of the world to enhance your potential. Meet new people, discover new circles, attend events, or join organizations. Experience new cultures, learn a new language or travel abroad or at least visit beyond your city and state. Embrace diversity and accept people's differences. Expecting others to think like you or act like you are signs of limitations in your own life. If you really want change, *you* have to change. True passion takes you beyond your experiences, neighborhood, degree and upbringing. It allows you to put your best foot forward to reach your destiny.

As I pursued my passion to help others, I gained valuable information to help people of all walks of life become financially fit. I've had the opportunity to teach financial literacy at schools and various organizations. I had the privilege of teaching the youth and adults how to save money, develop a budget and understand how credit works. Amazingly, the same communities where I once arrested the underprivileged, I taught how to gain resources for a better quality of life. In the beginning, I thought I was pursuing a job in the financial industry to learn more about financial health, but I learned so much more. It became clear that every single area in our lives affects the whole person.

My career path includes serving as a police officer, health and fitness trainer, inspirational speaker and financial specialist. Each step of this remarkable journey brought me closer to recognizing the bigger picture for my life. Today, I feel confident that my different positions were each another vehicle on my path to pursue what God created me to do. My diverse work experience gave me the knowledge and insight to meet the needs of the whole person. These experiences taught me how to help others live better at home, work, church and recreation.

Each step of this remarkable journey was another torch to ignite my passion for healthy living—spiritually, emotionally, physically, financially, socially, occupationally and economically. I discovered that becoming fit for God in *every* area in life is the key to navigate our way through society and take charge of our own health and economic success. During this incredible journey I discovered the true meaning of real success. True success is looking beyond yourself to empower someone else. Our greatest struggles become our greatest opportunities for strength. They give us a heart of compassion to be ready and willing to reach out and make a difference in the lives of others. Simply put, God blesses us to be a blessing! And my interdisciplinary expertise allows me to inspire all people to build healthy lives for their total well-being—inside and out.

And yes, my relationship with Morgan revealed my gifts that would lead to my passion. Morgan helped develop the healthy habits that would last throughout my lifetime. Our special relationship influenced my career and my future. Can you believe it? A dog was inspiration for my passion for physical fitness. Fitness led to my commitment to the whole person. Racing Morgan planted the seed where it all began. In school, I always excelled academically. But I didn't realize my athleticism until I brought Morgan home. My brothers played sports. But I was the only child in my family who ran track. And I was the only girl who had an active lifestyle.

Morgan was a great fitness partner. Then many years later when I grew up and had three children, I gained significant weight and struggled losing it. But healthy lifestyle practices combined with seeds planted in my early years helped me lose the weight and keep it off.

Years later a similar story unfolded when I got Nia for my daughter. LaTia was a cute chunky little girl with round plump cheeks. Children didn't play outside as much like we did as kids. After I brought Nia home, LaTia couldn't wait to come home from school to finish homework and take Nia outside. Nia was an energetic agile dog. She ran, played and jumped for hours it seemed. She kept both of us active. LaTia and Nia ran up and down the street, in the yard, and around the pond in our community. They played fetch and chase in the house. The more they ran and played, the fitter LaTia became. I've heard people say, "A tired dog is a happy dog." Well, a tired child is a happy child too. After they ran and played, they ate, then crashed from exhaustion.

During this time I was teaching fitness classes. And Nia knew "let's dance". When I put on energizing music, and said, "Let's dance, Nini", she jumped around on her two back legs with her front paws extended straight in the air. It was the cutest thing I had ever seen. And after years of teaching fitness, LaTia was finally inspired to join me when she saw Nia stepping to the beat. Nia kept energy and fun in the house. Her energy and playfulness encouraged LaTia to stay active. As my youngest, caring for a dog also taught LaTia responsibility and how to look out for the needs of someone else. These seeds followed her into adult life.

Years later LaTia would gain significant weight after having children. But she would get back on track with healthy habits she learned as a child. Running helped her lose the weight and keep it off. Healthy eating was a huge part of her fitness regime. Exercise puts you in a healthy mindset to eat healthy. She included more fruits, vegetables and whole grains in her diet. She avoided fried foods and fast foods and eliminated sodas and drank plenty of water. Sugary snacks and foods high in fat were limited. Exercise and moderation was key for a healthy life. Her personal struggle would ignite her passion to encourage others to live healthier. And yes, having a dog as a great fitness partner not only helped her become physically fit, Nia inspired her to discover her gifts.

So as you see, dogs can help you discover your passion and they make great fitness partners. And both human beings and dogs can take advantage of the many benefits of exercise. Even dogs get anxious, destructive or overeat when they don't get enough physical activity. In addition, health extends beyond the physical body. Dogs provide emotional health benefits too. They are fun, affectionate and always show unconditional love. The happiness they show you every time they see you is especially appreciated after a frustrating or stressful day. Their presence and comfort reduce stress, anxiety, and loneliness in children, young adults and especially older adults. Gently petting, rubbing and brushing a dog have a therapeutic effect that will calm and relax both of you. Plus dogs can help you stay positive as you pursue a healthy life.

Dogs don't complain, criticize or tear others down. They are so forgiving and they bring so much fun, energy and excitement in our lives. Dogs don't focus on the negative. They accept us as we are, but bring out the good in us. They remind us of the fun we had as children, without a care in the world. They make us laugh, which is one of the best medicines for our hearts. Dogs create so many positive experiences that will improve your mood and overall attitude as you strive to become healthy in every area of your life.

Life is so short. We should refuse to allow anything or anyone prevent us from having a happy healthy life. We should find every opportunity to surround ourselves with positive influences. We are not perfect, but with God's help, we can grow every single day. Connecting to positive people who are where you want to be or moving in the same direction will help you stay on track to achieve your goals. And yes, that includes our fury friends. Dogs uplift your spirit and make you happy inside!

CHAPTER 6
A LESSON FROM DOGS

What I find interesting is that d-o-g backwards is g-o-d. Is it possible that dogs convey a message that we need to carefully consider? Or does God reveal an aspect of Himself through our relationships with our dogs? If we pay close attention to their behavior, we can learn several life's lessons from dogs. Dogs can help us become better human beings. Caring for a dog teaches us patience, kindness, compassion, and forgiveness. We learn how to unselfishly love, how to give from the heart and how to care for the needs of another living being. I experienced these learnings as a young child while caring for different animals. Years later, these valuable life's lessons were repeated as my daughter cared for Nia.

When I brought Nia home, I was a young woman. As she got older I was moving into my middle-aged years. For nearly fifteen years, Nia was present during a critical stage of my spiritual growth. These years were challenging, as I faced many obstacles. Relationship issues, health and financial concerns, family medical crises and workplace conflicts battered my heart and mind. On top of that, my three daughters grew into young ladies and were faced with the realities of life. As a mother, one of the greatest pains I've endured is watching my children go through their growing pains.

My faith was tested on every side. Each new challenge seemed harder than the last. And at times I didn't know if I would survive the last crisis. Then one day as I was praying, Nia ran to me and nudged me with her nose. Then she tapped me several times with her paw. I got up and I looked at the time and realized it was passed her dinner time. She stared intently, while firmly pressing the front of her body on the floor. She was ready to take off like a sprinter racing to the finish line. Then she ran to the kitchen and grabbed her food bowl. Just as she anticipated, I followed her to the kitchen and fed her dinner. After she ate, she dashed to the front door, ready for her evening walk. When we finished walking, she stood on the front porch and stared at the door knob. She was sure that a comfortable bed awaited her on the other side. Before I completely opened the door, she dashed into the house, grabbed a toy and laid down in her favorite place. She didn't seem to have a worry or care in the world.

As I watched her, I realized that she had placed all of her cares in my hands. She was confident in my ability to take care of her. Obviously, dogs are creatures of habit. But habits are formed based on repeated behavior or what is experienced over and over again. My past actions supported Nia's routine. I thought, "Oh, God! A dog has more confidence in me, than I have in You." I was the intelligent creation who could think rationally, right? But after my prayer time, a dog had the answer to my worries, fears and concerns—to place all of my trust exclusively in God. At the very least, if I had the same level of faith in God that Nia had in me, life would be so much better. What an important lesson to learn from a dog. Can you imagine how God would feel if we place all of our cares in His hands?

As intelligent beings, I believe our ability to think in such detail is the very reason why we often fail to enjoy the true meaning of life. We have a tendency to try to figure things out. Overthinking the details of our existence leads to frustration, stress and ultimately worry. Worry can consume our thoughts, disrupt our lives and immobilize our minds. The ill-effect of worry damages our health and makes us less productive. This negativity feeds ill-feelings into our hearts and affects our environment and everyone around us.

Jesus teaches about worry in the Bible. He used the birds as the example. God created birds and He knows that they need food to eat. But birds cannot plant, harvest or store food in refrigerators, freezers, cabinets or barns. As they daily search for food for their families, they are solely dependent on God's provisions. God supplies their food and sustains their lives through the natural order of creation. If God cares about the birds, how much more does He care about human beings who were made in His image? The intent of Christ's message was to encourage total dependency on God. Worry is a deadly symptom of self-sufficiency. Worry happens when we focus on our ability, rather than trust in God's authority as our Provider. When we place our faith and trust in Him to supply all of our needs, we can conquer all worries, anxieties and fears.

Worry is one of our concerns. Another big problem is that human beings seem to never be satisfied. People often compare their lives, possessions, talents, gifts, and accomplishments with other people's achievements. If they don't compare, they feel like they don't have enough and need so much more. Obviously, if more was better, all rich people would be happy. And we know that's far from the truth.

Then people struggle with the poisonous effects of negativity. Some criticize others because it's really a reflection of how they feel about themselves. Others are so dissatisfied with their lives, they attempt to drag everyone into their pity party of despair. Still some live on emotional roller coaster rides, with their moods and attitudes fluctuating from day to day. Still, others are so unhappy that they fail to see the good in anything or anyone because they can't see the good in their lives. Then there are people in society who live vicariously through entertainers, stars and athletes. They seek to fill an empty void or avoid facing the dissatisfaction in their own lives. I believe this is one of the reasons why some people create false images of themselves on social media.

Have you ever thought what dogs would post if they had Facebook accounts? Would they use their accounts to criticize family members, friends or others? Would they complain about life? Or would they paint a false picture of their lives to impress others or to make themselves appear as a rising star? Or would they genuinely express the joy in their hearts to encourage others? Here are examples of what I believe Nia would post:

> Had another amazing meal.
> Had a great walk today.
> It was great to smell spring in the air.
> Jumped for joy when Mommy came home.
> Glad my bath and nail clipping are over.
> I feel and smell so much better.
> Got a new toy and had a yummy treat.
> I love my family and friends.
> I love playing fetch.
> I'm so glad to enjoy life!
> Oh my, I love the snow!
> Life is so dog gone good!

Watching dogs is a great opportunity to learn as we grow on our journey of life. Dogs rarely complain about anything. They take pleasure in the simple and ordinary events in life. Dogs appreciate the things in life that really matter. They are thankful for the attention, love and care. They appreciate spending time with family and friends. They know how to enjoy special moments, that humans take for granted.

Overbooked schedules in our hectic society snatch the joy out of living. Or we are so busy worrying about tomorrow, the past or the future we don't enjoy the day we've been given. Dogs don't worry about the future or get stuck in the past. They enjoy each moment. They eat every meal like it's the best meal. They treat every walk like it's the best walk. And every playtime seems like the best. They are happy when they wake up and they are happy when they go to sleep. Human beings tend to worry and wait for something more or better to happen. Dogs enjoy "right now".

During walks, Nia would pause and put her nose in the air to smell the cool breeze as it passed by. Other times she would stop and look around to enjoy the scenery. And whenever I brought bags in the house from the store, she excitedly leaped, anticipating a new toy or treat. If I didn't buy her either one, she still gave me a kiss and was glad to see me. She embraced every day like a special day. I've met people who look for reasons to be unhappy. Dogs find reasons to celebrate.

Nia brought so much joy into the lives of friends and family. They looked forward to our visits or visiting our home. Those experiencing difficulties and pain, shared how they always felt uplifted in Nia's presence. She was so in tuned to people's feelings and emotions, as she carefully studied others. If someone was sick or was experiencing the blues, she would perform a trick to make them laugh or smile. Then she affectionately placed her head in your lap or would rub her body against your legs to comfort your tears. People often said that Nia's love, personality and happiness was a reflection of the loving care she received over the years.

This is a major lesson I learned: If a dog's happiness is based on the love and care she received, should we be so much more elated? What if our attitude and actions were based on our confidence in God's immeasurable love for us? God loves us beyond measure. We were created because of His great love and absolutely nothing can ever stop Him from loving us. No circumstance, mistake, sickness or pain is so deep that God's love cannot reach down, heal us and pull us out. No problem is so big that God's incredible love cannot overcome it or knock it down. God's love is not based on our decisions or actions. He loves us in spite of us. His love accepts us just as we are, but His love makes us better day by day. His love is always present ready to help us, guide us, protect us and take care of us. His love enraptures our entire being to make us whole in every area of our lives. God's love is unlimited and eternal. Can you imagine how beautiful life would be if we fully embraced His love? We would overflow with so much joy and excitement that our genuine enthusiasm for life would be contagious and make a difference in the lives of others wherever we go.

Human beings were created as the pinnacle of God's creation. But have we given our role to the dogs? Are dogs outshining their human owners? Or is G-o-d speaking to us through our relationships with the d-o-g? As God's most intelligent creations, we should fulfill our life's purpose to the best of our ability. We were not created to complain, to spill the poisonous effects of negativity into our environment, or to belittle and criticize others. That behavior clearly dishonors God. We were created to encourage, support and to love one another. We were created to rejoice every day and to be thankful in all things. We were created to let our light shine, so others can see our good works and give honor to our Father in heaven.

When dogs have been given a task, they look forward to the challenge. Are you up for a challenge? Dogs can bark; but you can talk. It's time to live each day as a gift from God. Then let your words, actions and relationship with others reflect the excellence of a child of God. What a lesson to learn from dogs…Job 12:7 says, "But now ask the animals, and they will teach you; and the birds of the air, and they will tell you…"

CHAPTER 7
A DAY OF REMEMBRANCE

Nia was born September 10, 2001, the day before one of the most tragic days in American History. The following day, I vividly remember watching the morning news in the family room. On a clear Tuesday morning, a plane crashed into the World Trade Center in New York City. After the newscasters confirmed that the events were real; millions of Americans watched the events unfold. The twin towers collapsed and another airplane circled downtown Washington, D.C. The plane crashed into the Pentagon causing a devastating inferno and explosion. It was confirmed— America was under attack. I ran to the telephone to check on family members who worked for government agencies.

No one could get in touch with my niece who worked at the Pentagon. My family sat in prayer and anticipation, waiting for a call. It was unbelievable. We were directly affected by this attack on the nation. My niece was in the break room at work looking for supplies when she saw the breaking news. An airplane was in the wrong zone and circling downtown Washington, D.C. Then without warning, she heard a loud boom. The ground of the building shook like an earthquake. The lights went out and the next thing she saw was total darkness. All computer screens flashed a "911" emergency message.

Regular evacuation trainings taught her how to respond in an emergency. But she was surrounded by chaos. Both men and women panicked in the dark. Some employees' evacuation area had been hit by the plane so they ran in the opposite direction. My niece ran towards the stairs. Gripping the hand rails, she focused on keeping her balance while others fell. She felt like she was having an outer body experience because her body was moving while her mind was in a state of shock. She didn't know what was going on. Running to safety was the only thing on her mind. When they reached the outside door, it was forced opened by the crowd. Thick grey smoke filled the entire parking lot and sky. She could barely see anything and covered her nose. She made it to the meeting location for the department's head count. The division chief informed the staff that the plane that was circling downtown Washington, D.C. hit the Pentagon. The next sounds were loud screams, and the shout, "Run! Run! Another plane is coming!"

At this point, she was in survival mode. Her purse, cell phone, and other belongings were left behind. Three months pregnant with her first child, she wanted to make it home alive. Along with hundreds of people, she sprinted down the highway with all of her might. High heel shoes, jackets and other belongings were dropped and trampled by the crowds. My niece ran and ran, until she couldn't run anymore. Breathing heavily and gasping for air, she finally stopped to catch her breath. She looked up, saw a hotel and felt safe for the first time since the blast. Communication networks were down and cell phones didn't work. The hotel attendant saw the government I.D. badge hanging around her neck and offered the landline. She was able to reach her dad and he called the family to inform us that she was safe.

In the meantime, streets and major roads were blocked and traffic was deadlocked. No one could drive in or out of the city. Crowds of people were scattered throughout the streets of Washington, D.C. She walked for hours playing the event over and over in her mind. She was in total disbelief. She woke up that morning expecting to have a normal workday.

La Vita Weaver

She never imagined her life would be threatened and could have been taken away. Late that evening, metro trains were up and running again and she made it home safely. However, over 100 military personnel and civilians, including the 64 people aboard the plane died that day. The attacks didn't stop there. A California-bound plane was hijacked and crashed in a rural field in western Pennsylvania. The passengers learned of earlier events and fought the hijackers, possibly saving hundreds of lives.

On September 11, 2001 almost 3000 people died, thousands more were injured and billions of dollars in damage occurred during this terrorism attack on America. The death toll didn't stop there. Over 300 brave New York City firefighters lost their lives. Police officers, rescue workers, construction workers, and public volunteers carefully searched through debris of this heart-breaking mission. Some lost their lives searching for survivors or remains. People of different races, cultures, backgrounds and religions united and worked together. They lent a helping hand and risked their lives to rescue their fellow man. And we cannot forget our trusted and loyal companions. At least one hundred search and rescue dogs worked alongside their courageous owners to find trapped victims.

This event touched all of our hearts, either personally or as a nation. Then I thought, "What a message!" My niece's dad (my brother-in-law) and Nia shared the same birthday. But Nia was born the day before 9/11 and passed away April 22, 2016. The year of her fifteenth birthday, thousands of people gathered at Ground Zero after a decade and a half had passed of the horrific terrorist attacks on America. My family faced a close call, but my heart grieved for the people who lost loved ones, family members and friends. My heart goes out to the injured, to those who unselfishly risked their lives and to those who loved ones were never found. They are true survivors. They are surviving the grief, the pain and the heartache of this horrific event.

This day will never be forgotten. It's a day of remembrance. It's a day to count our blessings and to appreciate each day that we are given. It's a day to remember how people of different backgrounds, beliefs and cultures worked together undivided and can do it again. It's a day to remember to pray for victims and survivors and to pray for one another. I pray that God continues to surround the survivors with His amazing grace. I pray that His love, peace and hope will overflow in their lives. I pray that God will strengthen, heal and comfort their wounded hearts. The only way to survive this type of grief, is to trust in someone so much bigger and far greater. May God bless America! And may God bless the world with His everlasting presence!

CHAPTER 8
A COMFORT FROM ABOVE

Nia was never aggressive, only protective of family and friends. Naturally kind, gentle, and affectionate, her personality was a great comfort and support. Both family and friends shared how she brought so much joy and comfort during difficult times in their lives. She stared in people's faces trying to gauge emotions and feelings. I can attest to this fact. Over the years, Nia was sensitive to all of my concerns and brought comfort during tough years of my life. Until finally, she was no longer able to provide the care and comfort that was part of her nature.

One day in December, 2015, Nia sat on her favorite spot on the area rug in the living room. She intently stared at the wall, but there was nothing there. The large butterfly painting hung in the background. I thought that an image of Nia with my favorite picture would make an unforgettable photo. Then I asked, "Girlie, are you looking at the angels?" Something preoccupied her attention. This was the first time she stared for such a long period of time for no apparent reason. As I ran upstairs to grab my cell phone, she didn't budge. When I returned, she was in the same position and I took the picture. Then she immediately laid down on the edge of the carpet. That was the first and last time I would see Nia in that position.

Nia started having health problems earlier. But the beginning of 2016 is when her health started going downhill. Her quality of life quickly diminished. During baths is when I realized that her frail skeleton was hidden under plush fluffy fur. And the happy upbeat girl's personality was changing. The fluffy tail that once curled over her back hung lower than usual. This is when I knew her pain was intensifying. I carried her up and down the stairs to prevent falls. I got up several times during the night to take her outside to use the bathroom. Medication eased the pain and reduced diarrhea. And during vet visits she received intravenous fluids for dehydration. Regular vet visits and medication made me feel better. I was willing to do whatever it took to make her comfortable and to keep her alive. But it broke my heart to see this precious girl deteriorating. It was so hard to let her go. Either way it would be difficult and painful. Finally, I decided that I couldn't allow this beautiful dog to continue with such a poor quality of life. That would be so selfish and unfair.

I contacted family and friends because I knew Nia didn't have much longer to live. One by one people came to the house to visit. After LaTia and her kids visited is when I knew Nia was ready to go. Earlier that day, she had little energy and was lethargic. When she saw LaTia and her three children, she perked up. But I knew that she was tired and in pain. I had never seen a dog remain strong for others. But it made sense. Nia was very protective of LaTia and often treated her like a younger sibling. LaTia recognized that Nia's condition had rapidly declined in a short period of time. She cried and kissed her repeatedly. Then she said goodnight and left to go home. Right after I heard LaTia's car pull off, the next sound I heard was a loud thump. When I turned to see what hit the floor; it was Nia. She used all of her strength to see LaTia and the kids together for the last time. Then she helplessly crashed to the floor. She was stuck in that position from fatigue. I gently picked her up and carried her to the bedroom. She wouldn't eat or drink and she refused to take her medicine. And for the very first time in almost fifteen years, she showed her teeth. She was in so much pain and I knew it was her time.

The day Nia passed away was one of the most painful days of my life. I held her face in my hands as she intently looked into my eyes. I saw the compassion in her eyes as she stared deep into my soul. She was the one suffering, yet as usual, she was more concerned about my emotional state. I held back my tears and told her it was okay to let go. As I lovingly said goodbye, I kissed her cheek and thanked her for being such a beautiful, kind, loving and adorable girl. And it would be the last time I would address the "girlie in my worlie". Then I thanked God that Nia's purpose was beautifully fulfilled on this earth. She brought so much joy, love and comfort into the lives of family and friends. I thanked God for blessing my family with the pleasure of enjoying His precious creation for so many years.

Nia died peacefully in my arms, surrounded by so much love. I was thankful that she was no longer in pain. And for the first time in months, she relaxed in her favorite puppy position. Our eyes remained connected, even after she took her last breath. After I saw her chest rise and fall for the last time, I could feel my heart sink deep into my chest. At that moment, it felt like I could have lost my breath. That's how much it hurt. But I had to focus on the fact that she was no longer suffering and in pain. I had to remember that she had a good and happy life. I had to remember that she was well loved and shared so much love with others. These beautiful memories would remain a part of my heart forever. Instead of focusing on the pain of losing her, I had to hold on to the wonderful memories we shared with her.

As stated in the introduction of this message, I eventually tried to ignore the pain. I didn't know how to properly grieve for a dog. I knew people who lost family members and loved ones. How could I express these feelings to anyone? I felt so alone. Then I vividly remember the excruciating pain I felt when my father passed away. During that time, I prayed to God for help. I'll never forget the comfort that enraptured my heart like a warm blanket on a cold bitter winter night. I thought, surely He's the same God today. Scripture says that God cares about everything that concerns us. Matter of fact, He created Nia and He knew how much her death and life would affect my heart and emotions.

I began to openly share all of my memories, feelings, and pain with God. I didn't feel strange or uncomfortable telling Him exactly how I felt. I didn't feel awkward or weird telling Him how much I loved my precious girl. I shared whenever I thought about Nia, it felt like I had been hit in the chest and had shortness of breath. That's why I tried to ignore the pain. I freely expressed the inner depths of my heart with the One who had my heart in His hands. He created me and had the divine ability to comfort me. Then all of a sudden, it was like a damn broke and a flowing current of pain was released. I could not ignore it. I cried and cried and cried. I hadn't had a good cry in months. It was a good relief. I knew beyond a shadow of a doubt, that God was the One who truly knew the depths of my grief.

Grief is a normal part of life. Grief is defined as deep distress as if bereavement, or mourning, deep sorrow, sadness, or despair. Grief can be caused by the death of a human family member or a family pet. Or maybe you've experienced the devastation of the breakup of a marriage or the separation of a relationship. Or perhaps you have a financial crisis and lost your job or your home. Maybe a diagnosis of a serious health problem has caused sorrow in your heart. Or the trauma of some type of catastrophe or unexpected news has shattered your life. Everyone will experience grief at some point in life. But the question is: Where will you go for comfort?

Will you retreat into a cocoon and shut down from the rest of the world? Will you drown your sorrow in prescription medications; overindulge with food or an alcohol bottle? Will you blame yourself or others and allow anger, bitterness and resentment to take root in your heart? No matter what has caused the grief in your life, there is an answer. God is so close and He offers comfort during our times of distress. He is always there. And there is absolutely no tragedy so great that He cannot provide soothing relief and ease our pain. With God's help, He makes the pain bearable as we go through the process in time. He lovingly strengthens our hearts and gives guidance to endure all of life's difficulties and pain.

I had to accept my grief and acknowledge my feelings to be healthy and whole. No one likes pain. But I had to go through the pain, to grow through the pain. Today I know that it is perfectly healthy to grieve for a dog. Everyone will not understand our love for our pets. And it's okay. We don't have to explain our feelings, make excuses or get frustrated. What matters is that God understands the strong emotional bond we have with our fury companions.

And it's okay to cry for them. He loves them too. As a mother grieves with her child, He feels our pain and grieves with His children—you and I.

Writing my feelings on paper and expressing them to God was cleansing for my soul. I was able to grieve in a healthy way. It was healthy to have memories. It was healthy to have emotions. But I had to let go of the tears so I would not remain stuck in my grief. If we try to avoid the pain or don't deal with grief in a healthy manner it leads to anger, bitterness, depression, withdrawal and unhealthy habits. No matter the pain, we can release it to the One who created us and truly understands. That is exactly what happened. When I freely released it to God, there was an exchange. His presence comforted my heart and began to ease my pain. I felt a soothing peace and comfort flow through my heart. And during my intense travail, a tribute was birthed in memory of my precious girlie, Nia.

Days after I wrote Nia's tribute, I started meeting other people who lost pets. Many of them shared the same feelings. Pet owners and animal lovers could relate to the tribute. People who didn't have pets were moved to tears. Many of them shared the tribute with family, friends, neighbors and other community members. It was so nice to know that I was not alone. Or as one woman told me, "We animal lovers have to stick together."

Surprisingly, the family member who initially compared my relationship with Nia to possessions, said it touched her heart. She expressed she had no idea how much people genuinely love their pets. She encouraged me to share it with as many people as I could, so others can be comforted with the same comfort God placed in my heart. And that is exactly what happened. During difficult and painful times, God comforts us, so we can comfort others with the same comfort we received. He brings us out and blesses us to be a blessing. God *is* the God of *all* comfort!

CHAPTER 9
A HEALING OF THE HEART

Every human being will experience hurt, pain and disappointments. There are circumstances in life that are physically, emotionally and spiritually devastating. Pain, suffering, grief, and sorrow are part of our human existence on this earth. No one is exempt. No matter what we go through, God knows exactly how we feel and He really cares. I knew God really cared when I lost my dad. And He obviously cared when I almost lost my mom during her medical crisis and resuscitation. But I never imagined He cared so much when I lost my dog. I learned that there is nothing too small for God. And there is nothing too big that He cannot see us through it. Pain and heartbreak lead us to the One who cares the most. You learn that you don't have to go through it alone. God is right there. He is so close. It's something about the hurting that captivates the attention of God. His love, compassion, goodness and kindness goes out to the brokenhearted. Not only does He provide comfort in times of distress; He is the Healer of our hurting hearts.

Before I brought Nia home, I hadn't had a dog in over 10 years. This seems quite odd for someone who loves animals so much. Losing a dog was too painful and I didn't want to go through the hurt again. Years later, I only got Nia for my daughter's birthday. After our guinea pig Babyboy died, I knew that a puppy would bring so much joy and excitement in her life. Then after Nia died, I had no idea that other issues of my heart would arise. It was the first time in many years that I thought about my other pets. When my pets died in the past, I avoided thinking about them and didn't mention their names again. Instead of focusing on the joy of having them, I avoided the pain of losing them, especially as a child. The emotional distress was too much. And there was no one I could talk to about it. So I moved forward and put it behind me. So I thought.

Growing up, Morgan and I did everything together. When I brought him home, I remember thinking that "Mary" gave us Jesus who was a blessing to the world. And my mother's cousin "Mary" gave me Morgan, who was a blessing in my life. In no way did I place Jesus and Morgan in the same category. But it had a special meaning to a child. And I became curious about God at a young age. The many different species and varieties of animals aroused my curiosity about the God who created them. I started reading the red writing in the Bible because it talked about the "kingdom" of God. As a young child, I thought "kingdom" included all of the animals in the world.

Decades later, I would face Morgan's death. I remember asking, "God, are you kidding me?" I couldn't believe after so many years had passed by, I needed to cry over a childhood dog. Losing him was devastating. For all of those many years I blamed myself. I felt I should have saved him. When I came home from school, I saw a trail of blood leading to my bedroom. The trail led to Morgan lying helplessly in my bed. In those days, neighborhood boys shot animals with BB guns. They always shot at birds. Then I rescued cats and dogs that were abused by these same boys. Then one day someone shot Morgan when he was out in the yard. If only I had known that he was hit, my parents could have taken him to the animal hospital in time to save him. When he came into the house that morning after using the bathroom, he strutted through the door as usual. And then I headed to the bus stop to go to school. Finding him that way when I came home from school was an unimaginable image. He was lying on my side of the bed. I felt so bad that I wasn't there for him. He was shot with a BB gun and bled to death.

After I found him, I have no memories of what happened next. Everything else is a complete blank as if I blacked out. I was in total disbelief. Plus at that time, we were facing family crises in my household. So I blocked out the pain to survive. Or at least I thought I blocked it out. Unknowingly, these emotions help contribute to issues of the heart. Unresolved issues show up in different areas of our lives. When I began my journey of health and healing many years ago, I faced the pain of childhood issues, family crises, and broken relationships. I never imagined that facing the loss of pets would be a part of my process of wholeness. But it makes sense. It was unresolved pain. Our past hurt, pain and experiences influence our thoughts, emotions and how we respond to the world around us. Issues of the heart influence our choices, decisions and the direction our lives take. These issues of life shape and mold our character and influence our personalities. Now

I understand one of the reasons why I always felt the need to rescue others. I also learned why I was able to block out painful incidents, while people often assumed I didn't care. The opposite was true. I needed to be rescued and healed.

Only God knows the depths of what's really in our hearts. He understands how we have been deeply wounded and bruised by life's experiences. A child's traumatic experiences will manifest in other ways as we grow into adults. It's important that parents guide children through the healing process, even when they lose a pet. Children become very emotionally attached to their pets. My mom's cousin Mary was so nice and treated me very well. As I grew older, I always wondered why I no longer stayed in touch with her. The answer was revealed decades later. She gave me Morgan; so she was attached to a painful memory. Whenever I thought about Morgan, images of his death led to painful regrets in my heart. Finally, I released the pain and talked it over with God. Then for the very first time since Morgan's death, I remembered all of the good times we shared. I remembered how we ran and played together and had so much fun. I remembered how he was a good family dog. I remembered how my dad fed him steak from his plate. I remembered how Morgan especially loved my mom. And I was able to share these memories in this message. Facing the pain allowed God to heal this area of my life too.

We all have been deeply hurt and disappointed in life. Everyone has a story. I haven't met an adult who does not have a story of heartache and heartbreak. If not, the only thing they have to do is to keep on living. Childhood pain, family crises, rejection and relationship issues cause emotional turmoil and distress. Some people feel like running away or want to shut down and close off from the rest of the world. Painful experiences lead others to put up emotional barriers to avoid getting hurt again. But it's always there. Without healing, it doesn't go away and affects everything about us.

God wants to heal all of our unresolved issues of the heart. If not, they affect how we view ourselves and how we view everyone and the world around us. That's why we see people self-medicate to try to ease the pain. Others search for love, satisfaction and approval in all of the wrong places. Others focus on materialistic possessions, achievements, titles, positions, accomplishments or physical appearance to validate their existence and value. Then we see envy, jealously, low self-esteem, insecurities and competition. Other symptoms of a hurting heart are negativity, gossiping, criticizing and tearing others down.

Sometimes it can be learned behavior. Nevertheless, the root is the same. It began with someone's pain.

Signs of hurting hearts are seen in the home, at school, on the job and every place where people congregate. Verbal, emotional and physical abuse are culprits that lead to issues of the hearts. The results of pain within starts early in childhood. Bullies inflict their pain on others, without understanding their real issues within. We see micromanagers and workplace bullies use their title and position to intimidate others. Some overload people with unrealistic goals and expectations as if they are machines, rather than live human beings with a heart. They don't give others the same respect they desire, but treat others as inferior. They are never satisfied because the real anguish is within. Then some people have so much inner dissatisfaction that they see the worst in others. This is often a reflection of how they really feel about themselves. This behavior creates an unhealthy environment at home, school or on the job, which causes people to walk on eggshells to avoid criticism or confrontation.

Other hurting hearts are seen with people who are insensitive to the needs or concerns of others. Or they are easily agitated or angered, which leads to an explosive temper. Small things cause people who struggle with the inner turmoil of anger to explode. Still other painful events cause some people to develop a dominating personality. They control everything and everybody because they refuse to ever be disappointed or controlled again. Realistically, we live, work and socialize with people who see life through various colored lenses. Their view of others is based on their disappointments, pain and experiences, rather than embracing our differences. Managers, leaders, coworkers, family members and friends expect for others to function with their dysfunction. They often see everyone else as the problem. But their hurt within cries out loudly through their attitude, actions and behavior. They often fail to recognize their need for help and healing. Or they are afraid to face the pain and find it easier to focus on others.

And yes, there are people who prefer to invest their love and energy into pets, rather than deal with human relationships. They have been deeply wounded and disappointed by people, time and time again. Without healing from God, we all are pretty messed up. The saying, "Misery loves company." exists for a reason. Unfortunately, unhappy people tend to drag others into their pit of despair, even if it's unintentional. To the contrary, our pets create so many positive experiences in our lives. Pets laugh with you, play with you and comfort you. Our pets don't hold grudges and don't add unnecessary pain in our lives. You are free to be yourself because they accept you as you are. Pets don't criticize, put you down, gossip, complain, and fault-find or try to control you. They never share bad news and they are always happy to be with you. So it's easy to invest emotions into these precious creations. The only bad memory I have of my pets is their death. This is why losing them is so difficult. The good news is people who invest their love in animals are not closed off from others, as some assume. Their love for animals keeps their hearts open to the flow of God's love. But healing is needed to have loving relationships with people again.

Physical pain is a warning that something is wrong in our bodies and needs healing. In the same way, emotional distress is a sign that something in our hearts and lives needs healing. Don't ignore the pain. But you have to want healing for change. God wants to free those who have caused pain and the recipients of pain. He wants all people healed, healthy, and whole. And He wants us to love animals, but He created us to extend His love to all human beings. Undoubtedly, we all have been hurt. But God will guide us through the healing process. He wants us healthy and He wants us to have healthy relationships with one another. God doesn't want us to retaliate against those who have caused us harm. When we recognize that people are not the real enemy, we can pray for their healing too. It is no excuse to hurt others. The reality is: Hurt people hurt people; whether intentionally or unintentionally. Recognizing the need for healing is the first step to be free from these issues of the heart.

A big part of the healing process is forgiving those who have wronged us. If we look over our faults, mistakes and short-comings, we can forgive others knowing that God forgives all of our wrong doings. When we don't forgive, we remain in bondage to the perpetrator. Forgiveness is not so much for the other person, forgiveness sets us free. When we don't forgive, the unresolved issues of the heart is like spiritual heart disease that blocks the fullness of God's blessings. These blockages prevent God's goodness, kindness, love, patience, gentleness and compassion from freely flowing in our lives. It inadvertently affects our relationships with people everywhere we go. And the answer is not to cut people off; but to pray for the healing of us all. Then put your faith, trust and confidence exclusively in God. He will never fail you, disappoint you or put you to shame. He knows how to turn all things around for your good.

No one is perfect. God loves us in spite of our imperfections. And He wants us to love others in spite of their faults and weaknesses. We should forgive and love everyone; but we are not obligated to have everyone as part of our inner circle. We can choose to connect to people who desire to be healthy and whole and those who are striving for the same goals. We can choose to connect to positive people who encourage us, support us and help us grow. And yes, God wants us to encourage and support those who are struggling, but not at the risk of damaging our lives. Scripture says that two are better than one. When one falls, he can lift up his companion. On the other hand, bad company corrupts good character. We can ask God to show us how to have healthy relationships with those who harm us or practice unhealthy behavior. God may lead us to support them or to love them from afar. We cannot change other people's behavior, but we can control our response. And we can ask God to show us how to set boundaries to stay healthy and whole. We will never be perfect while on this earth, but we can live healthy and enjoy better relationships. As we grow in our relationship with God, He helps us have healthy relationships with others.

But the question is: Do you want healing? Then believe and have faith in God. Next, are you willing to do what it takes? In my past, I went through the process of healing over childhood pain and bad relationships. I never imagined that God would reveal pain I never faced as a child. It was buried in my heart. And when Nia died, it poured out like a flood. I saw Morgan and all of my childhood pets as if they surrounded me in the room. God helped the little girl nicknamed "Viti" who absolutely adored animals. I looked at each of them and uncovered the hurt within. But God was right by my side. And again there was a soothing exchange. When I released all of my feelings to Him, I felt His soothing presence begin to ease the pain. Then I was able to remember all of the good times I shared with all of my pets. Their lives were not in vain. They brought so much love, fun and laughter into my household. Each of my pets fulfilled a beautiful purpose in my life and made a difference in my heart. I was able to release more regrets and continue my journey of total-wellness.

When I started my journey of total health many years ago, I desperately wanted healing in every area of my life. I was in so much pain. I had nothing to lose, but I literally almost lost my mind. I struggled with binging, depression and overeating. I learned my struggle with binging and extra weight was less about what I was eating; and more about what was eating me. If I wanted change in my life, I had to do something different. I took a leap of faith and believed God would heal my heart, mind and total well-being. Then I put action into practice to make it happen. Of course I changed my diet and lifestyle. But in addition to exercising and eating healthier, I had to address the issues within that affected my outer world. I started praying again and reading the Bible daily, even if it was one scripture at a time. I fellowshipped with others to learn more about the Word of God and kingdom living. There is healing in the Word of God, but I had to open my heart to receive it. In addition, I connected to people moving in the same direction so we could encourage one another. Today, I've come a long way from where I started. I never imagined that I would be where I am today. It didn't happen overnight. It's a process and I've learned to enjoy the journey one day at a time.

During those years, I wrote my faith-based health and fitness book, *Fit For God: The 8-Week Plan That Kicks the Devil OUT and Invites Health and Healing IN*. Little did I know that health and healing would be a life-long journey. *Fit For God* was written over a decade and a half ago, when I was a younger woman in my thirties. However, the sound nutritional information, exercise tips, scriptures, prayer and praise are still relevant today. But I'm not the same. So much more healing has taken place in my heart. Today, I realize that my books, cd's, fitness programs, and all of my projects are like personal journals of my step-by-step process of wholeness.

Today I am so thankful for the changes that have taken place in my heart. I am so thankful that I am no longer in bondage to my past. I no longer see myself as a victim. I am a victor! I had to stop focusing on others and my outside world. I had to deal with the root of my poor choices—it was all about me. I had to stop the blame game and stop blaming bad relationships or people. I had to face my unhealthy choices and take responsibility for my own actions. And with God's help, I changed. A child is a victim, but an adult is a participant. Adults have a choice. I refused to get bitter and I chose to become better.

My pity party over past regrets had to go. I stopped focusing on the "if I should have", "would have" or "could have" syndrome. Or "Why did that happen to me and my family and kids?" Like our fury companions, we can focus on the "now". We can choose to make the best of everyday that we are given. Not only that, there is absolutely nothing we can do to change the past. Like Sodom and Gomorrah, our past has been disengaged in the flames and exists no more. It's over and done. Let's try to change the past. Think of the incident in the past you want to change. Put it in the forefront of your mind. Look at it. Now change it. Concentrate a little harder. Did it change? Absolutely not! You just wasted precious time and energy trying to change something you can do absolutely nothing about. Your effort could have been used more wisely to make life better today.

For decades I held on to the regrets of Morgan's death. I was so young, but I blamed myself. This unresolved issue took root and grew deep within my heart. As I grew into an adult, the issue of regrets spilled into every area of my life. Eventually, I sunk into a deep state of depression over life's regrets of childhood issues, failed relationships, family concerns, job choices and financial decisions. But thank God for healing my hurting heart. I'm so thankful that God was right there to safely guide me one step at a time. He doesn't reveal everything to us all at once. Only He knows what each of us can bear. He gradually reveals the areas where we need healing until we are completely free. And He knows when we are ready for the next phase of the process.

Not only did I learn to stop focusing on the past and life's regrets, I am no longer an enabler or a rescuer. I know my place as a created being. I'm only a messenger and a witness of what God is able to do because He has done it for me. Then it's up to the individual to want change bad enough to pursue it.

God is the only One who has the power to heal hurting hearts and change lives forever. But He gives us a choice.

During this process I also had to change my view and see life from a whole new perspective. I learned to see God in everything. And I learned that God is not a big bad disciplinarian waiting to whip us into shape. He created us with a free-will to choose to love Him and serve Him from the heart. And God never allows anything to happen to destroy us. That's why He sent His Son, Jesus Christ, so we can experience an abundant life in heaven and on earth. He plans the best for us, sees the best in us and hopes the best for us. God is the only One who has the divine ingenuity to work all things out for our good. Trials shape and mold our character. Difficult times allow us to experience that there is nothing greater than God's love for us. We see that He cares about everything that concerns us. Then we can share His love and goodness to give others hope during difficulties and hardships of life. My past regrets tried to suffocate my heart and immobilize my mind. But today I know that there is no one or nothing greater than God. With His help, I was able to put my past behind. And I look at past regrets as an opportunity to reach for God's best. My disappointments, pain, and poor choices led me to the One who could heal me and bring me out. Now I know that there is no limit to what I can achieve, even as a woman over fifty.

The most important difference in my life is experiencing God's freedom. I'm free from seeking to please others and I strive to please God in every area of my life. What He thinks is more important than anything. So thank God I'm free from myself, free from others, free from my past and free from society's views on success. True riches are not found in materialistic possessions, money, titles, accomplishments, popularity or positions. People often look for an outward breakthrough. The greatest riches are treasures in the heart. And I am so thankful for God's continuous flow of love, peace, joy, healing and hope that inspires me to enjoy the true meaning of life. And my passion is to encourage all people to pursue wholeness to live life to the fullest. God did it for me! And I want to share His amazing goodness, love, healing power and freedom with people everywhere. God wants to first work within us, to work through us. Will you take a leap of faith and trust God as your Healer? The psalmist said, "O Lord my God, I cried out to You, and You healed me" (Psalm 30:2).

CHAPTER 10
A BETTER LIFE TODAY

We love our dogs. They bring so much fun, joy and affection into our lives. But dogs have come a long way since biblical days. Ancient Israel had a different view of dogs. Dogs were not domesticated and were considered "unclean" animals. In many instances, it was acceptable for dogs to be badly beaten and horribly mistreated. Therefore the word "dog" was used as a term of humiliation. "Dog" was also used to describe a person who had a very low status or someone who practiced inappropriate behavior. A similar meaning is true today. When someone is called a "dog", it has a negative connotation. The word is associated with someone who is untrustworthy, abusive, offensive, mean or treacherous.

In our society, it would be unfair to view dogs in a derogatory way based on the past. In those days, certain groups of people were viewed differently. For instance, women were treated as second class citizens and didn't have the same privileges or value as men. Women could not legally own land or inherit their deceased husbands' property. If they had no husband or son, they were often left destitute or were at the mercy of the closest male relative. Other women resorted to shameful practices to survive or take care of their families.

If we view dogs badly based on ancient days, would it be appropriate to see women, the poor and people of different races, cultures and backgrounds in a similar way? How about people who made mistakes or suffer with diseases and certain medical conditions? In these cases, all of us would be outcasts and none of us would have a second chance. But Christ's love transcends all genders, cultures, and socioeconomic statuses. And I'm so glad God gives us another chance.

In the Bible Jesus referred to the term "dogs". During His teachings, He used illustrations that were relevant for that culture and time. This term painted a clear image of those who repeatedly refuse to embrace the teachings of God's kingdom. He conveyed a strong message that His audience easily understood, based on their view and treatment of dogs. Unlike the dogs of hundreds or thousands of years ago, dogs are domesticated today. Dogs roaming the streets, raiding trash cans or eating remains of carcasses are not common in our culture. Therefore, dogs are not seen as untamed wild animals today.

Dogs have earned the title as our cute, cuddly, faithful companions, friends and family members. Our "forever children" is an appropriate term to describe our relationship with our canine partners. Can you imagine? An animal that was once considered filthy and was badly mistreated is welcomed into our hearts and homes. The domestication of dogs gave them an opportunity to show their true value and worth as part of God's magnificent creation. Man was redeemed by God. Man has dominion over animals and redeemed the dog. And yes, dogs were bred by man. But God created and supplied the genetic material that produced the many breeds and mixes we enjoy today.

Today, having a dog is a major commitment. We spend much time, energy and money on their care. We feed, groom, walk and take care of our dogs. We provide the comforts of a home, buy toys, play fetch and teach tricks and commands. On the other hand, we get up early in the morning and go to work to pay our bills. Dogs don't. We buy groceries, clean the house, cook, wash laundry, or mow the lawn. Dogs don't. Unless the dog is a working dog, a house dog's primary role is to eat, poop, play, sleep and repeat. Would you agree that this relationship seems more beneficial for dogs? We earn a living and do all of the work. Yet they enjoy benefits of a comfortable lifestyle. Are they worth the investment?

Let's review some of the many benefits of our fury companions. Dogs give us the opportunity to fulfill God's desire for mankind to care for animals by welcoming them into our hearts and homes. Our pets keep the flow of love in our hearts which helps us extend love to our fellow human. These cherished companions are always there and remain faithful until the end. They are always happy to see us with the same level of excitement every single day. They bring so much laughter, fun, and joy into our lives. And a good dog for you fits your lifestyle and adapts well to your family's needs. Dogs are committed to their families and give unconditional love, affection and protection.

Our dogs remind us how dogs faithfully serve mankind and are part of the workforce. They protect the nation, keep us safe, rescue the loss, and guide and help those in need. Dogs can help children learn how to read and develop a healthy self-esteem. They teach children how to unselfishly give and care for the needs of someone else. And let's not forget those talented friends who have entertained us on television and in the movies over the many years.

Dogs make great fitness partners. Their nonstop energy and positive disposition help us live healthier. They keep us active and vibrant to feel better so we can live better. This positive relationship helps improve our overall well-being as we strive to become all that God created us to be. A lesson we learn from dogs is how to celebrate life. They teach us how to be grateful for every moment that we are given. They show us how to embrace our existence and focus on things that matter most in life. Our dogs don't worry about their lives. They show us how to trust God, as they exclusively trust in our care.

In addition, dogs present a day of remembrance for America. They remind us of those who lost their lives during the September 11th terrorist attacks on the nation. We remember to pray for peace, healing, comfort, strength and hope of the survivors and for those who lost loved ones and friends. Our faithful companions remind us of the one hundred rescue dogs and their courageous owners who searched through the debris to save lives. We are reminded how people of different backgrounds, races and cultures worked together for their fellowman and can do it again.

Last but not least, our relationships with our fury companions lead us to the Comforter and Healer of our hearts. The d-o-g on earth can help grow our relationship with the G-O-D of the universe. We can experience God's presence that gives us special care in our time of need. We learn that our Creator God is the *One* constant companion who will never leave us or forsake us. He is always there ready to help us, guide us, encourage us and strengthen us. You decide if dogs are worth the investment. We give dogs a good life; but the return is great. They help us live a better life today!

CHAPTER 11
A RELATIONSHIP BY GOD

In Chapter One of the book of Genesis, God shaped the earth and all creation in an orderly fashion. He made the moon, the sun and stars. He made the earth, the heavens and the seas. He made the birds in the air, fish in the sea, cattle in the field, and all living creatures on the earth. God looked at His magnificent works and said that it was "good". Mankind was made last of all creation. Therefore man could never boast or take credit for helping God create His magnificent works. Matter of fact, it clearly shows that God doesn't need man's help. He chooses to use human beings. Therefore, we should always humbly know our rightful place as a created being.

Man and animals were made from the same dust of the earth and they were given the same breath of life from God. But man was different than all other creations. The human race is the only creation made in the image and likeness of God. We have the ability to reason, make sound judgments and have moral standards. God doesn't have a physical body, but we were created to display His characteristics on the earth. We have the ability to reflect His kindness, patience, compassion, forgiveness, faithfulness and love. Man and woman were the crowning achievements of God's creative work.

After God created man, He gave him dominion over the earth and all of its creatures. Dominion is having complete authority and control over something. God is the Creator and Supreme Ruler of the earth. But mankind has the responsibility to exercise care of the environment and the animals. What an amazing privilege! It's an honor to be chosen as overseers of the Creator's masterpiece. Everything that God created was made for His good pleasure and glory. Nothing that He created was intended for bad purposes or inappropriate use. This includes the animals. Mankind should lovingly tend to the needs of animals and use them wisely for their intended purpose.

We see God's concern and care for animals in Scripture. Man's relationship with animals was established by God in the garden in Eden. God prepared a place to provide all of their needs and He placed Adam in the garden to tend to it. Then God brought the animals to Adam to see what he would call them. And whatever Adam called each living creature was its name. Why did God bring the animals to Adam? God created them and He could have named them. I believe God delegated this responsibility to show Adam's authority over them. Plus God showed Adam how He lovingly has authority over man. Adam's role was to watch over the animals with a loving hand as God cared for him.

Adam collectively or individually named the animals. Nevertheless, names gave them a unique identity. Not only that, it personalized the relationship and created a special bond. The animals were Adam's friends in the garden. We can relate to naming our companions and friends. Our dogs quickly learn their names as they respond to our call. We may choose names that are meaningful. For example, Nia was sweet-natured from the moment I brought her home. She was truly a beautiful dog, inside and out. We felt the name of a beautiful Hollywood actress was perfect. The actress would be happy to know that Nia wore her name well.

Parents can identify with the importance of a name. We choose names our children will be called for the rest of their lives. A name can be based on something or someone special. Personally, my first daughter's name means "joy". Seeing my first child for the first time was the happiest moment of my life. My middle daughter was named after one of my childhood cats (Oops, she may not want this shared). But this sweet Calico had a unique color pattern and was one of the most beautiful animals I had ever seen. I loved her dearly. Many years later, the same daughter named her daughter after my other childhood Calico. Ironically, my daughter never knew about this other cat. This was a strange coincidence. Then my youngest daughter was named after her father's youngest sister who was dear to my heart. Another irony is the name means, "aunt" in Spanish.

Regarding my name, my mom had little to no pain when I was born. I was her third pregnancy. Yet, she didn't know that she was in labor until her water broke. She had mild cramping, and then I quickly moved down the birth canal. My delivery was the quickest and easiest of the five children. My mother said I have been active, lively and on the move ever since. I was named, "La Vita", meaning "the life". As a child I preferred my nickname "Viti". I thought "La Vita" was a strange name for a little girl. Years later, people would say that "La Vita Weaver" was an artistic or inspirational name. Clients said it was befitting for an inspirational speaker who helped weave lives together. I never thought of my name that way before. After overcoming my personal struggles, I deeply desired to encourage others to live healthier in every area of life. Ironically, I once suffered with depression and wanted to die. That's a whole different story. Today I think that whenever someone called my name; they spoke life into my heart. Only God could have known my name would indicate my destiny in Him. In other words, I would live and not die (before my time) and tell others about God's incredible goodness and healing power. And now I absolutely love life and enjoy each day that I've been given! So names are important.

As Adam named the animals, he recognized that there was not a suitable helpmate among the animals for him. What I find interesting, is that God brought the animals to Adam before He brought Adam his wife. This is something to really think about. Before God established marriage or the family, he established the relationship between man and animals. Afterwards, God brought Adam his wife. Did naming the animals simply help Adam recognize his need for a suitable mate? Or did caring for the animals somehow prepare Adam for his wife and family?

Or maybe if Eve was present first, Adam would have been too distracted to care for animals. Similarly, do our relationships with our pets somehow prepare us for something greater? Or is it possible that God gave Adam the duty to name the animals because He had a greater plan and future for man and animals? We do not know all of the answers to these questions. But God's actions clearly show His love and concern for animals.

God's concern for the least of animals is illustrated in the Bible. Sparrows were the cheapest of creatures to buy on the market. They were not of any high value in the world. Two were sold for only a penny, the smallest copper coin. Yet Christ explained that one sparrow could not fall to the ground without His knowledge. If God cares about one sparrow falling to the ground, can you imagine how He grieves when animals are misused, abused, neglected, or mistreated? Proverbs 12:10 says, "The righteous man regards the life of his animal…." A person who seeks to please God considers the life of the animals and have compassion for them. They make sure the animals are properly cared for, fed and provided proper rest. Times have changed; but God remains the same. He still wants us to take care of His precious creations today.

CHAPTER 12
A CELEBRATION OF CREATION

God planted a garden and He appointed man to tend to the garden and to keep it. This garden was called "Eden", which signifies delight and pleasure. A beautiful plush landscape covered the garden and it was clothed with rich-colored grass and flowers. Fruit trees that were pleasant to the eyes filled its landscape. The garden's centerpiece was the tree of life, which sat in the midst of it. A flowing river watered the garden and divided into four riverheads, which contributed to the beauty and fruitfulness of the land. Nature furnished and adorned the magnificent landscape. Its ceiling was the heavens filled with the stars hung by the Creator's hands. The herbs of the land and fruit of the trees were man's food. This plentiful food from the earth was nutritious for the body and naturally delicious. Man and animals had everything they needed to live a healthy and fulfilling life. And they lived in peace with one another.

As parents plan and desire the best for our children, God created mankind to have a good life. God gave Adam and Eve a beautiful home, where all of their provisions were met and more. They would have need for nothing and would have no worries, fears or cares. They would enjoy genuine friendships with the animals. Can you imagine Adam rubbing the lions and tigers, while holding a precious lamb? Can you imagine Eve walking on a trail with the bears and being invited into their den? The greatest blessing is they had direct access to their Creator and God. He walked in the midst of the garden. What more could they have asked for? God only asked one thing. He commanded man saying that every tree of the garden he may freely eat, but of the tree of the knowledge of good and evil he shall not eat. Adam was given this command for his own good. Despite God's goodness and providential care, Adam disobeyed God and ate the forbidden fruit.

Mankind's disobedience led to painful consequences. Adam and Eve were banished from their magnificent home and would experience hardships on the earth. The fall of man affected everything that was under his authority, including the animals. For the first time, enmity and separation occurred between man and animals and they no longer lived together as friends. In the garden, animals were not used as food or clothing. Adam and Eve didn't realize they were naked until after their disobedience. Then they paid attention to themselves, covered their bodies with leaves, and hid from God. Later mankind would use the skin and fur of animals for clothing. Man's appetite would increase and he would eventually crave meat for food.

Despite man's fall, God's desire to save the human race is shown throughout the Bible. The story of Noah is another time when we see God's plan for creation. Years after the fall of man, the human race had become increasingly wicked. Noah was one of the few people who remained faithful to God's precepts. God instructed Noah to build a large ark, which was a vessel to save himself, his family and animals from the flood God would send to cleanse the earth. Two of each animals, and everything in which there was the breath of life, were placed in the ark with Noah and his family. Then it rained for forty days and forty nights, until the waters prevailed over the whole earth.

The story of Noah and the flood reveals both the judgment of God and His great compassion and love for all creation. Humans who lived apart from God's will died in the flood. The lives of those who had faith in Him were spared. Likewise, many animals on earth died in the flood. But those in the ark with Noah and his family were saved. Then God remembered Noah, and every living thing, and all the animals that was with him in the ark. And He made a wind pass over the earth, and the waters subsided. After almost a year in the water, the ark finally landed on dry ground.

The story of Noah shows God's desire for man and animals to be spared together. For almost a year, Noah and his family lived in the ark with the animals. God saved them from the flood's destructive force and they were chosen to replenish the earth. The story of the garden shows God's desire for animals and mankind from the very beginning. However, man was not created like robots to turn on or off at God's command or to be controlled like puppets on a string. God desired a family of people who would freely accept Him by choice. He wanted the human race to love Him on our own accord. Plus God is omnipotent or all-knowing. He knew in advance that Adam's disobedience would affect the entire human race and lead to a world of sin, suffering and pain.

What's interesting is that the Bible begins with the story of creation and man's life in the garden. It concludes with man's redemption and eternity in heaven. The Bible is like an instructional book to guide mankind back to the original purpose for our existence. One description of the acronym "b-i-b-l-e" is basic-instructions-before-leaving-earth. We were not created to handle the struggles, hardships and destruction of this present life. That's why we cannot survive this chaotic world's temptations, lies and deception without God's guidance and help.

Human beings were created for intimacy with God. We were designed to dwell in the midst of His bountiful goodness forever. The garden in Eden's picturesque landscape is like a blueprint of God's original design. It paints a clear image of His intentions for our lives. That's why the cares and temptations of this world easily lead people astray or make them feel downtrodden and hopeless. Some people pursue unhealthy relationships, possessions or accomplishments to overcome the inner turmoil. Life's heavy loads cause others to sink into depression. Still others rely on substances, overeating or medication to calm the anxieties within. Psalms 16:11 confirms that apart from God's will, everlasting peace and joy are impossible. It reads, "You will show me the path of life; in Your presence is the fullness of joy; at Your right hand are pleasures forevermore". We were created to have a life full of enjoyment and pleasure in the presence of our Creator. And God created a plan to bring us back to the original purpose for our existence.

This is when the concept of heaven is described. One description of heaven is a place where mankind who has been redeemed by Christ will spend eternity with God. Redemption is part of God's plan to rescue us from the penalty of sin. Jesus was the atoning sacrifice for the first Adam's disobedience. That's why Christ is called "the second Adam". He paid the price on the cross by shedding His precious blood. He willingly died for the sins of the world because of His immeasurable love for us.

This is great news for us; but what about the animals? I believe God has a special plan for animals. He placed them in the garden to enjoy its benefits with Adam and Eve. God saved animals in the ark with Noah and his family. Animals are mentioned in the Bible so many more times. A raven and a dove were sent from the ark to see if the flood waters had abated from the earth during Noah's day. And let's not forget the young donkey that Jesus road during His triumphal entry into Jerusalem during the Passover Feast. Imagine that: an animal had a role in our redemption plan. If animals served an important purpose for our Lord and Savior, Jesus Christ, they have to be good enough for eternity.

The reality is there is so much we won't understand or will know while we are here on this earth. But Scripture gives glimpses of heaven. In the book of John, Jesus told His disciples that He is going to prepare a place for them and He will come again to bring them to Himself. Commentators describe Jesus as referring to rooms in heaven where Christ's followers will live throughout eternity. Christ will one day return and take us to live with Him in heaven forever. We really don't know what eternity with God will be like. But if the garden in Eden's fabulous beauty and provisions provide a glimpse, we know that the place He is preparing is far better than any life we could ever imagine on this earth.

We are not sure of heaven's physical description, but we are certain that God will wipe away every tear; and there will be no more death, sorrow, or crying. And there will be no more sickness or pain. And thank God heartaches, worries, anxieties, and fears won't exist. These former things will all pass away. All of the wickedness and sins of this old world that caused so much destruction and suffering will be gone. God's people will live in a magnificent place that's described as a bride prepared for her groom. It will be pure, beautiful and radiant, ready to join her everlasting love. No physical description can compare to the indescribable joy and peace of living in God's presence throughout eternity. God's home will be among His people. What a glorious place!

Can you imagine? I imagine heaven as a place of celebration of God's magnificent creations. We will celebrate overcoming all of the temptations, hardships and pains of this world. We will celebrate our victory in Christ and being in the presence of the Most High God. We will celebrate the vision God planned from the beginning of creation. Every day will be a day to celebrate His goodness, His kindness, His compassion and His incredible love. Family members, friends, neighbors and all people who are overcomers in Him will celebrate united, as one family in God. All prejudices will be gone and there will be no more division of the human race. We will celebrate the victory of all God's people receiving His promises—a state of perfect peace, a new incorruptible body, and indescribable joy. We cannot imagine the full magnitude, beauty and radiance of our lives in eternity with our Creator and God.

A verse of the well-quoted *Lord's Prayer* says, "...Your will be done on earth as it is in heaven." Clearly, God does not want us to wait to get to heaven to live life to the fullest. He wants us to live each day like heaven is for real. That means every day is an opportunity to celebrate the gift of life. Every day we can look forward to something more beautiful than anything we can ever imagine. Every day we can rejoice knowing that this life is preparing us for a far better place. Every day we should love one another, embrace each other differences and treat others with the same respect we desire. We should strive to become better every day, as our lives reflect the amazing promises of God. As children of God, our lives should reflect heaven as a glorious place of celebration filled with God's goodness and greatness. Then we should pray daily for God's perfect will to be established on earth, as it already is in heaven.

And if heaven is beyond what we could ever imagine, why wouldn't animals be there? Our limited knowledge and wisdom can never understand the full scope and measure of God's incredible plan for all creation. Think about this: God gathered dust from the earth, formed it, breathed life into its nostrils and created something great—the human race. Surely He has a plan for animals. They are part of His magnificent work too. I firmly believe with no doubt that animals will be in heaven. Brilliantly arrayed with fabulous colors and unique characteristics, they display the majestic work of our Creator's hands. The intricate details of their design and attributes reveal the infinite beauty and awesomeness of our Creator's mind. It's too hard to believe that these magnificent beings were created to disappear and be forgotten forever.

Then what about our family pets? The Bible does not reveal if our pets go to heaven. On the other hand, it doesn't give evidence that they will not be there. Since man earned a place in heaven by honoring God, will dogs and other pets earn a place beside their owners for honoring man? Will these beautiful creatures have the privilege of spending eternity with the ones they helped the most? Or was their purpose fulfilled on the earth? What we know for certain is that Jesus is preparing a place for those who have faith in Him. What type of home is He preparing? Will heaven be filled with the best of this life that brought us so much joy, combined with all that we cannot imagine? Will that include our pets that are so dear to our hearts? Has our relationship with animals on earth prepared us to spend eternity with animals in heaven?

As an adult, I've often thought about my mother's sacrificial love for her children. For instance, she felt so much compassion when she saw my joy and love for animals. She put aside her own feelings and allowed me to bring animals into our home, as part of the family. The way I see it, if my earthly mother's heart was touched by my love and relationship with animals, surely my heavenly Father cares so much more. His great love for us and the animals is unfathomable. Plus He knew from the very beginning how animals would be used in amazing ways to touch our hearts and lives.

Interestingly, animals served a major role in my life. My love and care for animals would reveal my life's purpose. Rescuing animals and nursing them back to health, prepared my heart of love and compassion for people who are hopeless, hurting, and brokenhearted. Today, I whole-heartedly share God's incredible goodness, hope, healing and love with people of all walks of life, races, cultures, and nationalities. Similarly, the responsibility of helping to take care of Nia prepared LaTia for her future. She gained the patience and tender love to care for the sick and dying as they prepare for eternity. And we both were inspired to help people live healthier to become all that God created them to be. In conclusion to the whole matter:

God works all things together for our good. And there is so much about His future plans that is a great mystery. But we can be sure that He will do exceedingly, abundantly, beyond all that we can ever think, ask or even imagine.

You may still wonder, "How can animals go to heaven when they are not part of God's redemption plan?" Unlike human beings, animals don't have the ability to follow God's commandments or make moral decisions. Therefore, animals cannot choose salvation, right? But consider this: God is the Supreme Ruler and Creator of the entire universe. As the *only* omnipotent One, He can do whatever *He* chooses for His good pleasure. Animals were placed in the garden without a command. Surely, God can place them in heaven without a salvation plan. Adam was given the commandment. The sin of the human race destroyed God's original creation. Therefore, man needed a salvation plan. Animals were under man's authority and were affected by his fall.

The garden in Eden reveals God's vision of man and animals living in paradise in harmony with one another. And if everything had gone as God intended, man and animals would have never died. They would have remained in the garden forever.

If animals were part of God's original plan, why wouldn't they be part of eternity? One day God will restore everything anew. There will be a new heaven and a new earth; free of the corruption of the evil deeds of this world. Restoration includes God's magnificent creations living as He intended from the very beginning.

Maybe you are still wondering if dogs were only meant for our enjoyment and pleasure while on this earth. All of our questions won't be answered on this earth. In the meantime, we have something to think about. What's important is to enjoy our pets and celebrate their existence while they are with us. And we can treasure the precious memories of our pets that have passed away. Nia faithfully served her purpose on the earth. But when I get to heaven, I won't be surprised, when I'm greeted by a host of God's creations and my "forever Nia" hopping in the crowd. I know *dogs gotta be in heaven!* My sincere hope and prayer is that you are absolutely certain that you will be there.

Today, I still miss Nia so very much. But I can smile when I think about the joy she brought in my life and the lives of so many others. Many people have described Nia as a beautiful and special dog. But what was also special about Nia was her unique marking. Black and tan Shiba Inus have similar markings. And I think it's absolutely adorable that the tan patch on their chest resembles wings. But the tan pattern on Nia's chest was distinctly shaped like butterfly wings. And everyone who knows me knows how much I love butterflies! I have butterfly jewelry, books, dvds and more. Plus a large butterfly painting hangs on the wall in my family room, which was Nia's favorite place to spend time with loved ones.

I find the butterfly so intriguing because its existence is evidence of the miraculous work of our supremely intelligent Creator. And there is no compelling evidence that this magnificent creature once existed as a lowly caterpillar. If God used His infinite wisdom to create an intricate plan for an insect; surely He uses hard places in our lives like cocoons to prepare us for our destiny. The butterfly's incredible transformation gives us hope. When we place our faith in God, we become new creations to enjoy a brand new life. Then at the appointed time, we are released to take flight and reach higher heights, as we fulfill *His* purpose for our existence.

What I find most surprising about this butterfly message is that I had Nia for nearly fifteen years; but this distinguishable mark was not noticed until after her death. Apparently, that was the right time. When a dear friend recognized it in a photo, I was astounded. Then I remembered how butterflies captured my attention after I brought Nia home. Apparently, the butterfly that covered Nia's heart connected to my heart long ago. And seeing the image after Nia's death was comfort and confirmation to hold on to the promises of God. It's amazing how God's wonderful creations conveyed a remarkable message that would change my life forever.

In my conclusion, Nia's wings are symbolic of a heavenly purpose on earth. And as I changed from the inside out, her work was almost done. Then the radiance of heaven's smile that connected our hearts, called my angel home.

Therefore, Nia's tribute is a celebration of experiencing one of God's precious and beautiful creations. Like a woman in labor, only an amazing God has the divine ingenuity to birth something beautiful out of so much pain. And just imagine…if our pets are used as such amazing blessings in our lives, how much greater are God's plans for you and I?

A SPECIAL TRIBUTE

Dogs Gotta Be In Heaven
A Loving Memory of A Companion & Friend

Who can understand the love between a companion and friend…
A love that never fades away and remains faithful until the end
No matter how often you leave the house and no matter the time
You're greeted by a wagging tail, a leap of joy, and a genuine smile

A bond that always celebrates your presence and total well-being
If you feel down, she puts her head in your lap to comfort your pain
She knows your moods and daily routine better than you know yourself

When you're tired, she grabs your slippers and encourages you to rest

A special stare only meant for you; that gleam in her beautiful brown eyes
It uplifts your spirit with tears from heaven that makes you joyful inside
She is so appreciative for this special bond and for all that you have done
She returns companionship, devotion and the greatest is unconditional love

This special relationship of mutual joy combined with all of her daily kisses
It's pure and sweet without any motives; it captivates your heart's attention
It's as though she feels every heart beat and is connected to your very soul
A feeling you cannot explain to everyone, only God and animal lovers know

I'm convinced God allows this incredible bond between companion and friend
A special gift to enjoy and celebrate the magnificent work of the Creator's hands
These were my precious memories, as I held Nia's face and looked into her eyes
She stared straight into my soul, I held back my tears and peacefully said goodbye

Dogs Gotta Be In Heaven

I thanked her for the many years of joy she brought to my friends and family
A sweet, smart, cheerful, loving and adorable girl; well-loved by so many
Nia's suffering ended she passed away in my arms in her favorite position
I kissed her cheek and thanked God for this time with *His* beautiful creation

The pain was severe as though I lost a family member; and I really did!
God's presence comforted my heart and I felt how much He really cares
Since I was a child I always wondered why do I love animals so very much
God needs people to care for the animals, so He placed the love in our hearts

Today, I feel so blessed that I had this amazing experience
With this type of love, only sent from above, I know...*Dogs Gotta Be In Heaven!*

July 18, 2016

Dedicated to my precious girlie, Nia, "Nini" September 10, 2001 to April 22, 2016

ABOUT THE AUTHOR

La Vita Weaver is an inspirational speaker, *author*, fitness trainer, and CPR instructor. She is the author of the faith-based health and fitness book *Fit For God*, and shared the joy of fitness as co-host on the popular *TBN* show "TotaLee Fit", with 8-Times Mr. Olympia. La Vita presents life-changing messages at workshops, conferences, and special events across the nation. Her interdisciplinary expertise allows her to inspire all people to build healthy lives for total wellness—spiritually, emotionally, physically and financially. La Vita's genuine enthusiasm and joy for life is contagious!

To schedule a workshop or speaking engagement or for more information contact:

(844) Fit-4God
(844) 348-4463
Or Visit www.FitForGod.com
(Download brochure/tribute)

Dogs Gotta Be In Heaven
P.O. Box 151442
Alexandria, VA 22315
(703) 763-7678

www.ingramcontent.com/pod-product-compliance
Lightning Source LLC
Chambersburg PA
CBHW071704040426
42446CB00011B/1910